First World War
and Army of Occupation
War Diary
France, Belgium and Germany

17 DIVISION
Divisional Troops
78 Brigade Royal Field Artillery
12 July 1915 - 31 March 1919

WO95/1991/3

The Naval & Military Press Ltd
www.nmarchive.com
Published in association with The National Archives

Published by

The Naval & Military Press Ltd

Unit 10 Ridgewood Industrial Park,

Uckfield, East Sussex,

TN22 5QE England

Tel: +44 (0) 1825 749494

www.naval-military-press.com

www.nmarchive.com

This diary has been reprinted in facsimile from the original. Any imperfections are inevitably reproduced and the quality may fall short of modern type and cartographic standards.

© **Crown Copyright**
Images reproduced by permission of The National Archives, London, England, 2015.

Contents

Document type	Place/Title	Date From	Date To
Heading	WO95/1991/3		
Heading	17th Division 78th Brigade R.F.A. Jly 1915-Mar 1919		
Heading	17th Division 78th Brigade R.F.A. Vol I 12-31-7-15		
War Diary	Winchester	12/07/1915	12/07/1915
War Diary	Havre	13/07/1915	13/07/1915
War Diary	Bayenghem	18/07/1915	18/07/1915
War Diary	Campagne	19/07/1915	19/07/1915
War Diary	St Sylvestre	20/07/1915	23/07/1915
War Diary	Dickebusch	24/07/1915	31/07/1915
Heading	17th Division 78th Brigade R.F.A. Vol. II August 1.15		
War Diary	Dickebusch	01/08/1915	31/08/1915
Map	Ref Sheet 28 1/20000		
Heading	17th Division 78th Brigade R.F.A. Vol 3 Sep 15		
War Diary	Dickebusch	01/09/1915	05/10/1915
War Diary	Near Steenvorde	20/10/1915	25/10/1915
Heading	17th Division 78th Bde. R.F.A. Vol. 5 Nov 15		
War Diary	Near Ouderdom	06/11/1915	24/11/1915
Heading	17th Div 78th Bde. R.F.A. Vol. 6		
War Diary	Ouderdom	09/12/1915	10/12/1915
War Diary	Ypres	11/12/1915	31/12/1915
Heading	17th Division 78th Bde. R.F.A. Vol. 7 Jan 16		
War Diary	Ypres	01/01/1916	02/01/1916
War Diary	Ochtezeele	03/01/1916	03/01/1916
War Diary	Audenfort	04/01/1916	31/01/1916
Heading	78th Bde. R.F.A. Vol. 8		
War Diary	Audenfort	01/02/1916	06/02/1916
War Diary	Buysscheure	07/02/1916	07/02/1916
War Diary	Steenvoorde	08/02/1916	08/02/1916
War Diary	Ypres	09/02/1916	29/02/1916
Heading	78 R.F.A. Vol 9		
War Diary	Ypres	01/03/1916	12/03/1916
War Diary	Caestre	13/03/1916	23/03/1916
War Diary	Armentieres	23/03/1916	18/05/1916
War Diary	Vieux Berquin	19/05/1916	19/05/1916
War Diary	Bayenghem Lez Seninghem	20/05/1916	30/06/1916
Heading	17th Div. XV. Corps. War Diary Headquarters 78th Brigade, R.F.A. July 1916		
War Diary	Fricourt	01/07/1916	24/07/1916
War Diary	Dernacourt	25/07/1916	31/07/1916
Heading	17th Divisional Artillery. 78th Brigade Royal Field Artillery August 1916 Ammunition expenditure. Casualties.		
War Diary	Dernancourt	01/08/1916	01/08/1916
War Diary	Montauban	02/08/1916	20/08/1916
War Diary	Bonnay	21/08/1916	22/08/1916
War Diary	Allonville	23/08/1916	23/08/1916
War Diary	Occoches	24/08/1916	24/08/1916
War Diary	Gaudiempre	25/08/1916	29/08/1916
War Diary	Bienvillers	30/08/1916	31/08/1916
Miscellaneous	78th Brigade R.F.A.	01/08/1916	01/08/1916

War Diary	Bienvillers	01/09/1916	05/10/1916
War Diary	Hebuterne	06/10/1916	16/10/1916
War Diary	Pas	17/10/1916	17/10/1916
War Diary	Albert	18/10/1916	29/10/1916
War Diary	II/I Thiepval	30/10/1916	31/10/1916
War Diary	Thiepval	01/11/1916	30/11/1916
War Diary	Ginchy	01/12/1916	10/12/1916
War Diary	Meaulte	11/12/1916	11/12/1916
War Diary	Morlancourt	12/12/1916	26/12/1916
War Diary	Ginchy	27/12/1916	03/03/1917
War Diary	Carnoy	04/03/1917	04/03/1917
War Diary	Albert	05/03/1917	05/03/1917
War Diary	Martinpuich	06/03/1917	16/03/1917
War Diary	Albert	17/03/1917	17/03/1917
War Diary	Albert & Puchevillers	18/03/1917	19/03/1917
War Diary	Beauvoir Riviere	20/03/1917	23/03/1917
War Diary	Boubers	24/03/1917	24/03/1917
War Diary	St. Michel	25/03/1917	25/03/1917
War Diary	Bray	26/03/1917	31/03/1917
War Diary	Arras	01/04/1917	12/04/1917
War Diary	Monchy	13/04/1917	15/06/1917
War Diary	Arras	16/06/1917	16/06/1917
War Diary	Gavrelle Plouvain	17/06/1917	27/06/1917
War Diary	Gavrelle	28/06/1917	30/06/1917
War Diary	Gavrelle Plouvain	01/07/1917	11/07/1917
War Diary	Gavrelle	12/07/1917	29/07/1917
War Diary	Gavrelle Plouvain	29/07/1917	14/08/1917
War Diary	Gavrelle	15/08/1917	28/08/1917
War Diary	Gavrelle Plouvain	29/08/1917	26/09/1917
War Diary	St. Nicholas Anzin W/lenis	27/09/1917	30/09/1917
War Diary	Arras	01/10/1917	01/10/1917
War Diary	Herzeele Belgium	02/10/1917	02/10/1917
War Diary	Nr. St. Sixte	03/10/1917	03/10/1917
War Diary	Langemarck	04/10/1917	08/11/1917
War Diary	Elverdinghe	09/11/1917	09/11/1917
War Diary	Proven	10/11/1917	10/11/1917
War Diary	Noordpeene	11/11/1917	26/12/1917
War Diary	Ribecourt	26/12/1917	06/01/1918
War Diary	Hermies Havrincourt	07/01/1918	11/01/1918
War Diary	Hermies	12/01/1918	28/02/1918
Heading	17th Div. Headquarters 78th Brigade, R.F.A. March 1918		
War Diary	Hermies	01/03/1918	31/03/1918
Heading	17th Divisional Artillery War Diary 78th Brigade R.F.A. April 1918		
War Diary	Senlis	01/04/1918	06/04/1918
War Diary	Englebelmer	07/04/1918	26/05/1918
War Diary	Beausart & Engelbelmer	27/05/1918	30/06/1918
War Diary	Corbie	01/07/1918	14/07/1918
War Diary	Senlis	15/07/1918	31/07/1918
Heading	17th Divl. Artillery 78th Brigade. Royal Field Artillery, August 1918		
War Diary	Senlis	01/08/1918	12/08/1918
War Diary	Morcourt	13/08/1918	19/08/1918
War Diary	Mesnil	20/08/1918	25/08/1918
War Diary	Courcelette	25/08/1918	28/08/1918

War Diary	Martin Puich	29/08/1918	29/08/1918
War Diary	Flers	30/08/1918	31/08/1918
War Diary	Lesboeufs	01/09/1918	06/09/1918
War Diary	Fins	07/09/1918	25/09/1918
War Diary	Heudecourt	25/09/1918	27/09/1918
War Diary	Gouzeaucourt	28/09/1918	29/09/1918
War Diary	Gonnelieu	30/09/1918	05/10/1918
War Diary	Vauchelles Wood	06/10/1918	08/10/1918
War Diary	Selvigny and Caullery	09/10/1918	09/10/1918
War Diary	Ligny and Inchy	10/10/1918	10/10/1918
War Diary	Inchy	10/10/1918	20/10/1918
War Diary	Neuvilly	21/10/1918	23/10/1918
War Diary	Ovillers	24/10/1918	24/10/1918
War Diary	Poix du Nord	25/10/1918	04/11/1918
War Diary	Futoy	04/11/1918	05/11/1918
War Diary	La-Tete-Noir	06/11/1918	08/11/1918
War Diary	Limont-Fontaine	08/11/1918	15/11/1918
War Diary	Haucourt	15/11/1918	07/12/1918
War Diary	Manancourt	08/12/1918	08/12/1918
War Diary	Meaulte	09/12/1918	09/12/1918
War Diary	Pont Noyelles	10/12/1918	10/12/1918
War Diary	Allery	11/12/1918	28/02/1919
War Diary	Allery (Somme)	01/03/1919	31/03/1919

W2957/1991 (3)

17TH DIVISION

78TH BRIGADE R.F.A.
JLY 1915-MAR 1919

17th Division

121/6401

78th Brigade R.F.A.

Vol. I

12-31-7-15

Nov '19

Army Form C. 2118

78th Brigade RFA
17th Division

WAR DIARY
INTELLIGENCE SUMMARY
(Erase heading not required.)

July 1915

Place	Date	Hour	Summary of Events and Information	Remarks and references to Appendices
WINCHESTER	2/7/15		78th Brigade RFA 17th Division marched from to Southampton on night of 11th and 12th July 1915 (Lt. Col. E.H. WILLIS Commanding) embarking as follows:- 4 Batteries and Head Quarters on S.S. NIRVANA. The first unit arrived at Quay 6 a.m. and all aboard by 10.45 a.m. 12.7.15. Ammunition Column on S.S. MOUNT TEMPLE arriving at Quay 7.14 a.m. and all aboard by 10 a.m. 12.7.15.	4
HAVRE	13/7/15	8 a.m.	S.S. NIRVANA at Quay side HARVE 8.a.m. 13.7.15 and all were disembarked by 11 a.m. S.S. MOUNT TEMPLE at Quayside HARVE 10.30 a.m. 13.7.15 and all were cleared by 12.30 p.m.	
HAVRE	13/7/15	5.30 p.m.	All units entrained for BAYENGHEM commencing at 5.30 p.m. 13.7.15 and all detraining at WIZERNES last unit arriving at bivouac at 7 p.m. 15.7.15	
BAYENGHEM	16/7/15	9.30 a.m.	Brigade marched to CAMPAGNE arriving in bivouac at 2.30 p.m.	
CAMPAGNE	19/7/15	9 a.m.	Brigade marched to St SYLVESTRE arriving in bivouac at 3.25 p.m.	

Army Form C. 2118

WAR DIARY
or
INTELLIGENCE SUMMARY
(Erase heading not required.)

78th Brigade R.F.A. July 1915

Instructions regarding War Diaries and Intelligence Summaries are contained in F.S. Regs., Part II. and the Staff Manual respectively. Title Pages will be prepared in manuscript.

Place	Date	Hour	Summary of Events and Information	Remarks and references to Appendices
ST SYLVESTRE	20/7/15	4 pm	Brigade inspected by General Sir Herbert Plumer. Comd'g 2nd Army	
"	23/7/15	7.45	Brigade marched to 3rd Division area S.W. of YPRES and bivouacked East of REMINGHURST. Am' Column remaining at ST SYLVESTRE till 24th when it moved into own area	
DICKEBUSCH	24/7/15	9.30 p	Our Section pm battery observed a section of 28th F.A. Bgd L. in action north of DICKEBUSCH	
"	25/7/15	9.30 p	Brigade completed taking over from 28th Brigade, and is attached to 3rd Division and affiliated with 9th Infantry Brigade. O.C. Bgd. 'Droghan-Smith'.	
"	26/7/15		Batteries registered their fronts. Enemy's aeroplane detected C battery firing, & ranged a 5.9 howitzer on it at 5.30 pm. Good practice, but no casualties. C/81 (Howitzer) co-operated with 78 Brigade in the Right group and Lt Colonel P.H. Wilkin Front covered St ELOI & WYTSCHAETE-VIERSTRAATWEG	
"	29/7/15	3.30 pm	Three letters 461 - 478 - 0/78 howitzer shelled the HOSPICE in the afternoon, the place containing many parties of the general behind our lines.	
"	31/7/15	2.30 am	Shelled enemy's working parties returning work in front of Trench Afforte 02-03.	

121/6753

17th Kwain

78th Brigade R.F.A.
Vol: II
August. 15.

Army Form C. 2118

WAR DIARY
or
INTELLIGENCE SUMMARY
(Erase heading not required.)

August 1915   78th Brigade R.F.A.

Place	Date	Hour	Summary of Events and Information	Remarks and references to Appendices
DICKEBUSCH	1.8.15		Brigade in action 1 mile south of DICKEBUSCH. 52nd Infantry Brigade took over the line ST ELOI to WYTSCHAETE – VIERSTRAAT road during night of 1st/2nd August as follows: 10th LANCASHIRE FUSILIERS – trenches M1 to N1. 9th WEST RIDINGS N2 to N5. 12th MANCHESTERS N6 to O4. 9th NORTHUMBERLAND FUSILIERS P1 to P4/5	
	2nd		with a composite reserve made up of all 4 Battalions. Brigade transferred to 17th Division in noon. Communications with Battalions at present unsatisfactory, mainly owing to fact of having 4 Battalions in front zone instead of 3 as at first.	
	3rd		Quiet day — a few "test" fired. Lines not very good owing to failure of communication.	
	4th		Batteries registered on own active particular zones. D Batt. fired 5 rounds of shrapnel at enemy working party over P.2.	
	5 & 6		Quiet days. Communications considerably improved — but would be much better if a more liberal supply of instruments were issued. Trenches have been dealt with to taping underground cable between each Batt. Ken Infantry Headquarters. Should to a great improvement.	
	7th		B Batt. fired 8 rounds at German support trench in retaliation to fire on our Infantry C/B/31 but 12 hydrated into a dump to WYTSCHAETE RIDGE suspected to be a German O.P.	
	8th	2 am	A Batt. was called upon to support an attack upon front of German lines. Effect reported very satisfactory.	

Army Form C. 2118

WAR DIARY
or
INTELLIGENCE SUMMARY
(Erase heading not required.)

Aug. 1915   70 F. Bell R.F.A.

Place	Date	Hour	Summary of Events and Information	Remarks and references to Appendices
DICKEBUSCH	9.8.15	2.30am – 3.15am	Bombardment was carried out by Right Group (less 1 section M/78 + 1 section C/78 attached to Group under Col Cardew as "counter battery"). The Bombardment was in cooperation with an attack made by Troops on our left to regain lost trenches at HOOGE: Assisted in conformance with 1st R.A. orders No. 8" (late 2.7.15). A + B Batteries fired at German Fire Trenches, C. Batt. at communication trench and remaining section of S/78 + C/78 at reserve trench. As a result a trench of 80× was made in the German front trenches. about 200× west of PICCADILLY FARM (O8a.2.7.) After entanglements was totally cut about. The Germans subsequently made 2 attempts to repair this trench but in each case the working parties were dispersed by shrapnel fire. During the bombardment a F.O.O. located the flashes of a German battery in O.13.d.9.4. This target was afterwards engaged by A, B + C Batteries.	Appendix I.
	11.		The enemy made an attempt to repair PICCADILLY FARM but were dispersed by fire from B/178 + C/7th.	
	12.		Infantry report that there seems to be fresh troops in front of them and that considerable activity has been shewn in enemy repairing trenches + parapets. Several rounds were fired at enemy working parties with good results. It is also reported that the enemy have brought up fresh heavy artillery. 2nd Lt E.C. Dampft R/178ms slightly wounded in the thigh this evening by a rifle bullet when he was up at the O.P.	

1875 Wt. W593/826 1,000,000 4/15 J.B.C. & A. A.D.S.S./Forms/C. 2118.

Army Form C. 2118

WAR DIARY
or
INTELLIGENCE SUMMARY

(Erase heading not required.) 78th Bde R.D.A.

Aug 1915

Place	Date	Hour	Summary of Events and Information	Remarks and references to Appendices
BIEKEB-SCH.	13.8.15	about 5.30	The enemy shelled 15/78: the first two rounds fell about 150 yds behind No 2 gun, about 20 rounds were very accurate, one shell exploded in and last few rounds very accurate and badly damaged the gun carriage. The gun was removed by the Salvage Corps later in the evening. The Siege of the shell was "8.2"	
	14.8.15	9.15 am	The enemy again shelled 15/78 with a few rounds and again about half later got about 40 more near the Battery. The men were got away to one side and no damage was done except to some of the dug-outs in the interval a Batt fired 37 rounds in answer to the infantry call. They were being shelled. When it got dark by the infantry night to Batt took up a new position. Book to the left of its former position	
	15.	1-1.30 pm	The enemy fired about 20 little shells from BIEKEBUSCH, damaging several the west side of the Batt. P46 of the Salvage Corps	
		6 pm	A few rounds were fired to assist the infantry who were being shelled on the Battlines being carried of. The enemy stopped immediately.	
			The trenches in front are now held by the 9th Inf. Batt. & are being taken over tonight from the 16th Lancashire Fusiliers at present the 75th Bde. At Manchesters and 9th Northumberland Fusiliers. The disposition of the 75th Bde regiment of the battalions on P1 — P4G to P46 to night.	

M1 — N3
N4 — O4
P1 — P4G

J.B.C. & A. A.D.S.S./Forms/C. 2118.

Army Form C. 2118

WAR DIARY
or
INTELLIGENCE SUMMARY
(Erase heading not required.) 78th Brigade R.F.A.

August 1915

Place	Date	Hour	Summary of Events and Information	Remarks and references to Appendices
KEMMEL	17.8.15	9pm	Enemy very lively bombing and shelling our trenches first when reliefs were accomplished. Batteries replied vigorously and after a considerable expenditure of ammunition silenced the battle fire. Very small allotment of ammunition given to Right About two weeks. this using caused two of the Batteries to exceed their allowance	
	18.8.15		2nd Lieut H.J.A. Abrams was posted to A Battery vice 2nd Lieut E.C. Dunfee evacuated to England.	
	19.8.15		Communications with trenches very irregular. The manual to patrol their post of the line cannot be cable lines from all Batteries are nearly completed regularly. New O.P. If properly looked after should prove very satisfactory. which	
	21.8.15		All quiet on our front - heavy guns behind WYTSCHAETE fired a large number of rounds on YPRES	
	22.8.15		Enemy working parties very active engaged on making new trenches round HOLLANDSCHESHUUR FARM.	
	23.8.15		A + C Batteries fired 12 rounds each on new enemy trenches between BUS QUARANTE and HOLLANDSCHESHUUR FARM - at the same time 9BR fired 12 H.E. on the communication trench which she shooting was watched and the results poor.	

WAR DIARY
or
INTELLIGENCE SUMMARY

(Erase heading not required.)

Army Form C. 2118

78th Brigade R.S.A.

August 1915

Place	Date	Hour	Summary of Events and Information	Remarks and references to Appendices
DICKEBUSCH.	25.8.15.		German working parties opposite N 6 were observed engaged on support trenches in rear of PICCADILLY FARM. Fire was opened on the target apparently with effect.	
	26.		900 rounds shrapnel was allotted to 78th Bde this week. But with the exception of an occasional working party, good targets have been very hard to find. Enemy aircraft have been very active between 8 and 10 am the last two mornings.	
	27.		The D. 5. cattle lines to the trenches have been completed and are working well.	
	28.		About 120 rounds were fired on German communication and support trenches and other likely points. At 5.30 pm a concentration of all batteries on one point was tested; some hostile fire much too long to get their rounds off. The 105 West Yorks (50th Bde) relieved the 7th Borders in P1 – P4b on the night of the 27/28th.	
	29.		Enemy guns have been very quiet except in D Battery's position and the enemy generally puts about 6 crumps into the position about 10 in the morning. The enemy has been apparently searching for the trench with another howitzer shell. A/B 4th come into action in front of C/81 and are grouped with the 78th Brigade; serving Brigade Headquarters through C/78B. are connected by telephone to Brigade Headquarters	

Army Form C. 2118

WAR DIARY
or
INTELLIGENCE SUMMARY

(Erase heading not required.)

78th Brigade R. F. A.

August 1915

Place	Date	Hour	Summary of Events and Information	Remarks and references to Appendices
VICKEBUSCH	3.8.15		35 rounds fired by B/78 and 27 by C/78 on enemy communication trenches. 3 enemy howitzer shells fell close to C/78 this morning.	
	3.8.15		About 30 rounds in all fired by C/78 and C/81 at enemy working parties over N trenches. The enemy seem to be using a new gun with which they shelled a Battery's old position and a field gun near VICKEBUSCH today: fragments picked up the shell seem to have an immense piercing nose and a long fuze.	

Edward Sr. F. Colonel
Comdg 78th Brigade R.F.A.

Sketch Map showing Principal Points in Right Group Zone

Ref Sheet 28 1/20,000

121/7050

17th Division

48th Brigade R.F.A.
Vol 3
Sept. 15.

WAR DIARY or INTELLIGENCE SUMMARY

Army Form C. 2118

September 1915   7? F.A.B.

Place	Date	Hour	Summary of Events and Information	Remarks and references to Appendices
BIKERNIECH	1.9.15		B/78 fired 44 rounds on 2 enemy machine guns located by infantry and attacked them. In the evening enemy succeeded the but in front of C/78 with 10.2 cm shells: our search for unit in front of No 3 gun C/78, totally damaging its carriage. The gun was removed when it became dark	
	3.9.15		Very quiet all along the front — the enemy shelled the by the BRASSERIE at intervals. The infantry have gone away by destroying there; and by constructing large towers apparently to get a view of the enemy	
	4.9.15		A & C/78 and A/78 fired 24 rounds each on a suspected whereby gun position and A/78 quick onto fortunate enemy O.P. in attacked and horse Battery which several enemy groups about 6 pm apparently standing by the train	
	5.9.15		Acting on orders from Group Commander A/78 × C/78 fired 70 rounds shrapnel and C/78 to A.E. in enemy works from HOLLANDESCHESCHANS FM to BORS QUARANTE which have been in age. Several direct hits were scored but the result was very disappointing for the enemy's trenches hardly damaged at all.	
	6.9.15		Much other from 7 D.A. took tallying the enemy Eb trenches were attack but in a front position (In make active) Their guns are seen on guns another brigade sent into action. 2 small round on still	

Army Form C. 2118

WAR DIARY or INTELLIGENCE SUMMARY

(Erase heading not required.)   78th F.A.B.

Instructions regarding War Diaries and Intelligence Summaries are contained in F.S. Regs., Part II and the Staff Manual respectively. Title Pages will be prepared in manuscript.

September 1915

Place	Date	Hour	Summary of Events and Information	Remarks and references to Appendices
DICKEBUSCH	6.9.15		Hit the church in object like enemy putting out of the enemy forfeit opposite guns hty M.L, was hity not (a) but and sent a burst on it - apparently without doing any damage.	
	8.9.15		Very quiet the attacks gun well registered on various targets.	
	10.9.15		Twice they enemy working parties were observed near GREY ROME J HOUSE they were fired at and dispersed.	
	12.9.15		Enemy working parties have been fired at near S.W corner of BOIS QUARANTE. German 8.2" howitzers have been lively yesterday, to rounds fell along the VIERSTRAAT road to the left of C/81 and to-day over 50 rounds were fired at C/78 (150×h left front of ----B/78) the shooting was erratic and no damage was done	
	14.9.15		Several new enemy working parties were dispersed at various points by enemy shrapnel fire.	
	15.9.15		In the morning enemy working parties were dispersed near PICCADILLY FM. About 4 fm. an aeroplane letting fish one salvo at an unseen target was and mostly observed all shots were short to except fire at 10-40 am and whereby the 2 guns abord N.5.c.6.2 and shelled VIERSTRAAT with intermittently throughout the day.	
	16.9.15		Enemy rather active shelling RIDGE WOOD and VIERSTRAAT with shrapnel.	

Army Form C. 2118

WAR DIARY
or
INTELLIGENCE SUMMARY
(Erase heading not required.)

78 F.A.B.

September 1915

Place	Date	Hour	Summary of Events and Information	Remarks and references to Appendices
DICKEBUSCH.	17.9.15		C/78 and C/81 fired in conjunction on WYTSCHAETE - VIERSTRAAT RD behind the enemy's line. C/81 fired several rounds and stopped the enemy bringing the A.M. trenches about 10 p.m. Enemy aeroplane over us dropping at RIDGE WOOD and round WILTSHIRE FARM.	
	18.9.15		C/81 fired a few rounds in retaliation to enemy batteries firing on HOOGE. A British aeroplane was brought down by rifle fire this evening and landed near A/78. The machine was only slightly damaged.	
	20.9.15		20.Ty F.A.B. are going to cover the infantry on our right. B/78 in reserve relieving A/78 in this position. The relief of one section took place last night. Several targets were registered by this section. A.Day.	
	21.9.15		3 rounds fell about N3 & S 7 about 4.30 pm. Each shot was afterwards claimed by a hostile aeroplane.	
	22.9.15	4-5 pm	Bombardment of enemy's line and C.M.E. trenches was carried out according to 17 D.A. orders. The shelling was good + our H.E. seemed very effective. The enemy parapet was totally knocked about in several places. No demure was used on stonework was fatal fully destroying enemy's reply with whizzbangs and C.M.E. trenches mainly on our C.M.E. trenches and VIERSTRAAT. small H.E.	

Army Form C. 2118

WAR DIARY or INTELLIGENCE SUMMARY

(Erase heading not required.)

78 F A B

September 1915

Place	Date	Hour	Summary of Events and Information	Remarks and references to Appendices
RIDGE WOOD	23.9.15		Last night the remaining section of A/78. This morning about 7.30 the enemy shelled the left section with Whizbangs. Enemy replied with RIDGE WOOD with the portion of PETIT BOIS suspected to have reserves in it. The Bombardment was again carried out during the 4 & 5 pm. The was directed on the section of the enemy trenches near PICCADILLY FARM. 70 H.E. and 165 shrapnel were fired by the 78th F.A.B. and 20 H.E. by C/81. The light was good.	
	25.9.15		But the fire seemed effective. In cooperation with an attack on HOOGE this morning Bombardment was carried out from 4.20 to 5.10 am on the enemy's front trenches and chrapnel CME support trenches in our own zone. 360 rounds of was fired by 78 F.B. and 25 rounds by C/81. Between 9 was 11 am first was opened by our own batteries in retaliation to enemy guns firing towards HOOGE.	
	26.9.15		Very quiet till about 10.15 pm when heavy firing started up at HOOGE. At first it was reported to be an attack by the enemy and orders from 17 D.A. A and D/78 and C/81 opened fire in counter batteries and the "sunken road". The enemy's firing gradually dropped and all quiet by 11.15 pm.	

1875 Wt. W593/826 1,000,000 4/15 I.B.C. & A. A.D.S.S./Forms/C. 2118.

Army Form C. 2118

WAR DIARY
or
INTELLIGENCE SUMMARY

(Erase heading not required.) 78 B. F.A.B.

September 1915

Instructions regarding War Diaries and Intelligence Summaries are contained in F. S. Regs., Part II. and the Staff Manual respectively. Title Pages will be prepared in manuscript.

Place	Date	Hour	Summary of Events and Information	Remarks and references to Appendices
DICKEBUSCH	27.9.15	5.30 pm	Enemy fired 6 4.2" shells which fell near C/81 cutting the telephone wires: no aeroplane was seen observing the shots:	
	28.9.15		Some 5.9 shells fell during the morning between C/81 and C/78 no damage was done: again the evening aeroplane appears to be watching	
	30.9.15		Fairly quiet all along any aeroplane observation our front.	

Neville Holmer
Maj. 78 Brigade R.F.A.

Army Form C. 2118

vol 4
78 RFA

WAR DIARY
or
INTELLIGENCE SUMMARY
(Erase heading not required.)

78th F.A.B.

October 1915

XVII

Place	Date	Hour	Summary of Events and Information	Remarks and references to Appendices
DICKEBUSCH	2/10/15		Yesterday & today have been very quiet, on allotment of ammunition being very limited. Enemy shelled the VIERSTRAAT road in front of 9/78 with a few heavy shell about 4 p.m. no damage was done	
	3/10/15		Orders were received this morning (17 DAN/24; 3.10.15 – appendix 1) for the relief of 78th Bde by West hams Div. The relief of the first section to take place this evening by 11.30 p.m. for A.C. y D Batteries.	
	4/10/15		The day was spent in registering the relieving sections of West hams Artillery – one section of B/78 was relieved this evening by one section of the 13th West hams Battery.	
	5/10/15		Light was bad & little registration was done – the remaining sections of all batteries were relieved this evening. BCs handed over command of batteries on completion about 8.30 p.m. The C.O. & B.Cs stayed till 12 noon 6/10/15 to give relieving officers any assistance they could: the rest of the 78th Bde moved straight into rest billets at NUNROCH near STEENVOORDE, where the CO & BCs proceeded the following afternoon.	

Breeze Colonel
Commanding 78th Brigade, R.F.A.

Army Form C. 2118

WAR DIARY
or
INTELLIGENCE SUMMARY
(Erase heading not required.)

Place	Date	Hour	Summary of Events and Information	Remarks and references to Appendices
near STEENVOORDE	20.10.15			
	21/10/15		Orders were received this evening that the 107th & 109th Batteries (23rd Brigade 3rd Division) would be relieved on the evening of the 22nd by two batteries of 78th F.A.B. B/78 & C/78 were ordered to relieve these batteries respectively. Battery commanders of B & C/78 went forward to reconnoitre their positions	
	22/10/15		B & C/78 (accompanied by their second line ammunition wagons from the Amm Col) went up to 23rd F.A.B. wagon lines about G.24.b.8.8. (Sheet 28 NW 1/20,000) Relief of guns &c. was carried out this evening, 252 rounds of ammunition being dumped at the guns. The positions are :- B/78 I.19.b.4.5. & 2 guns of C/78 I.15.a.2.1. & 2 at I.15.a.5.2. B/78 are grouped with 80th F.A.B. under Lt Col Carlew & C/78 with 79th F.A.B. under Lt. Col. W. E. Anderson.	
	24/10/15		H.Q. 78th F.A.B. & A & D Batteries moved up to remaining wagon lines of 23rd F.A.B. (about G.24.b.8.8.)	
	25/10/15		Amm Col 78th F.A.B. moved into new billet at G.19 & 88	

17th Buraun

78th Bde: R.F.A.
VSR: 5

12/7656

Nov. 15

Army Form C. 2118

WAR DIARY
or
INTELLIGENCE SUMMARY
(Erase heading not required.)

HEADQUARTERS
70th BRIGADE, R.F.A.

Month: November 1915

Place	Date	Hour	Summary of Events and Information	Remarks and references to Appendices
near OUDERDOM	6		Lt. Col. E. H. Willis took command temporarily of the Right Group vice Lt. Col W.E. Anderson.	
	12		Right Group relieved 46th F.A.B. Headquarters Right Group are now at I.1.6.6.2 (Sheet 28) at C/78 position. 79th F.A.B. I.2.d.3.9.	
	19		One section of A/78 went into action at J.2.d.1.1. The other section of A/78 and the whole of D/78 should have gone into action at the same time but were prevented by heavy shell fire. D/78 lost 2 men gunners killed.	
	20 24		Remaining section of D/78 went into action this evening at J.1.d.7.5. A and D/78 are grouped under Col. W.E. Anderson commanding Left Group.	

S.P. Leiver L.
Adjt for O.C. 7 Fd Bde.

78t Bde. RFA.
tot: 6

121/7910

17 fébr.

WAR DIARY
or
INTELLIGENCE SUMMARY

Army Form C. 2118

78 F.A.B.

December 1915

Place	Date	Hour	Summary of Events and Information	Remarks and references to Appendices
OVERSON	9th & 10th		Lt. Col. E.H. Willis and the 78th Bde H.Qrs. staff returned and took over the left group which comprises the 78th Bde H.Qrs. and the following batteries: A/78 C/78 D/78 B/79 C/79 D/79 The whole zone covered by left Group extends from BELLEWAARDE FARM to Mt Kemble (inclusive). Area Tuesday one occupied by 51st Bde. The Group H.Qrs. is at the junction of the YSER and YPRES canal. Most of the telephone lines through parts of YPRES and in the winning are constantly shelling, the lines are frequently being broken.	
YPRES	11.			
	12		Headquarters dug out are situated by the continual rain to which they are built below. There is no attempt to be stopping into the stream below. We are possible place for Headquarters; the dugouts have been drawn up as far as possible, and also new drains dugouts made after the side of the bank	

WAR DIARY or INTELLIGENCE SUMMARY

Army Form C. 2118

Place: YPRES
December 1915   78 F.A.B.

Date	Hour	Summary of Events and Information	Remarks and references to Appendices
13	2.30 p.m	A bombardment of enemy trenches and strong points was carried out today in conjunction with H.A.R. and 6th Siege. About 200 H.E. and 200 rounds shrapnel were expended. The shooting seemed successful on the enemy's trenches and works and apparently badly damaged. The enemy retaliated but not apparently vigorously. Considerable artillery activity by the enemy on various points.	
14.			
15.	1.30 p.m	In conjunction with H.A.R. and Howitzer bombardment at slow rate of fire were carried out on the enemy support trenches during the 5th Brigade tour. A and D/78 fired: 50 rounds H.E. and shrapnel being expended.	
17.		Enemy shelling has been unusually severe last two days	
19		About 5.15 am this morning gas was very heavy shelling on the 6th Division on our left. At the same time heavy clouds of gas (chlorine) drifted down from the north-east — many officers and men were affected the fumes while they were asleep or before they had	

WAR DIARY or INTELLIGENCE SUMMARY

Army Form C. 2118

(Erase heading not required.)

December 1915   78 F. A. B.

Place	Date	Hour	Summary of Events and Information	Remarks and references to Appendices
YPRES	12		realised the danger and put on their gas helmets. The enemy was shelling all round YPRES particularly the roads, they also began searching along the canal bank by the camp headquarters and finally put one shell by the telephone dug out killing one man and smashing all telephone wires. All the staff were suffering from the effects of the gas and were very exhausted. Steps were taken at once to mend the wires but it was not till late in the afternoon that general communication by telephone could be reestablished. In the meantime by the slowness of all information the batteries carried on ; doing on their own and managing every communication themselves. The fire was extremely accurate and reported by the infantry as afterwards. Though the shelling of the batteries was very bad and the heavy work on gas helmets had been badly and the officers and men exhausted. The men still were fired at A/78 carried on gallantly. But 200 gas shells C/78 men position and considerable damage was done to material C/78 men though this was no actual harm to confinemento now	17

WAR DIARY
or
INTELLIGENCE SUMMARY

78 F.A.B. December 1915

Place	Date	Hour	Summary of Events and Information	Remarks and references to Appendices
YPRES	22		heavily shelled. a sergeant was killed by a direct hit and one gun emplacement and Lt Lloyd was badly wounded in the arm. By 9 am the drift gas had cleared away sufficiently for smoke helmets to be taken off. Information was obtained from the "King's Westminster" of the 6th Division that a feeble enemy attack had taken place on their front and had been frustrated. Enemy's fire slackened somewhat during the day but increased again in the evening especially on 6th Division area. Communication with all batteries was established by 7 pm and orders were given to batteries to be on the alert. About 11.30 pm a false report coming through Div. Signals stated that 51st Bde front was being gassed. Enemy barrage roads throughout the night but with gas shells at intervals throughout the night lost few were the casualties amongst the transport.	
	23		No further drift gas sent over probably because wind had veered more to the West. Enemy shelling much less severe in the morning and from gas shells were used	

WAR DIARY or INTELLIGENCE SUMMARY

Army Form C. 2118

78 F.A.B. December 1915

Place	Date	Hour	Summary of Events and Information	Remarks and references to Appendices
YPRES	23		but in the afternoon the whole of the KAMP without again was heavily shelled when it became the enemy shocked out by midnight everything was quiet. Situation normal. Some of the batteries dug outs are still uninhabitable on account of the gas in them.	
	24			
	25th		Christmas Day. There has been very little hostile fire to-day and our front line has been exceptionally quiet.	
	26th 27th		} Quiet.	
	28th		This morning was quiet but the wind gradually moved round to S.E. and in the afternoon YPRES and its approaches were heavily shelled between 2 p.m. and 3.30 p.m. A considerable number of 26 c.m. and 42 c.m. shells were used by the enemy. In the evening a large number of lachrymatory shells used by the enemy formed quite a formidable barrage on main approach to YPRES. The wind changed to the South at about 8 p.m. and the hostile artillery ceased its activity.	
	29th		YPRES was fairly heavily shelled at about midday.	
	30th 31st		} Quiet.	

Sd/ ……
Lt Colonel Commanding, 78th F.A.B.

78th Bde: R.F.A.
No: 7
Jan. 16

17th Division

WAR DIARY or INTELLIGENCE SUMMARY

Army Form C. 2118

January 1916.

Place	Date	Hour	Summary of Events and Information	Remarks and references to Appendices
YPRES	1st.		Quiet day on Left Group front. Relief of 17th Div by 24th Div commenced. Knight section wagon lines of T8th Bde. R.F.A. moved at 8a.m. to WEMAERS-CAPPEL - OCHTEZEELE - ARNEKE - LEDRINGHEM - ZERMEZEELE. Taking over ordnance guns & equipment of 107th Bde. R.F.A. About 6p.m. personnel of right section of 107th Bde. took over positions, guns & equipment from 78th Bde. Personnel of right section of 78th Bde moved to above area by motor bus.	
	2nd.		At 6 a.m. enemy trenches were bombarded with Trench mortars in conjunction with all batteries of the left group. Batteries commenced firing 15 secs after the trench mortars finishing a barrage on CME Trenches for 3 mins. They then stopped for 2 minutes repeating this operation four times. Enemy did not reply to our bombardment this day. Remaining sections of wagon lines of 78th Bde. R.F.A. moved at 8 a.m. to the above WEMAERS-CAPPEL - ARNEKE - ZERMEZEELE area taking over remaining guns & equipment of 107th Bde. At 6 p.m personnel of 107th Bde. took over positions, guns & equipment from 78th whose personnel left by motor bus for above area.	
OCHTEZEELE	3rd.		78 Bde. marched at 8.15 a.m. via WATTEN - NORDAUSQUES - BONNINGUES to rest billets at CAHEN - CLERQUES - HAMEL - AUDREHEM - LE POIRIER arriving at Headers at 4.30 p.m. Billets were allotted as follows: - 78th Bde. H.Q. - AUDENFORT C/78 HAMEL A/78 CAHEN D/78 CLERQUES B/78 AUDREHEM AC/78 LE POIRIER	

Army Form C. 2118

WAR DIARY
or
INTELLIGENCE SUMMARY

(Erase heading not required.)

January 1916

(21)

Place	Date	Hour	Summary of Events and Information	Remarks and references to Appendices
AUDENFORT	4th 5th 6th		Bde. occupied in arranging billets, checking & cleaning equipment.	
	7th to 11th		" "	
	12th		Inspections carried out by Bde. Commar. of all equipment, personnel stores.	
			78 Bde. less C/78 carried out route march & was inspected on route by Brigadier Gen. R.W. Ouseley C.R.A. 17 Div. Art.	
	13th		C/78 marched CALAIS to carry out experimental practice in wire cutting.	
	14th to 17th		Batteries carried out skeleton drill orders, gun laying drill, marching drill, signalling, N.C.O.'s + laying examinations.	
	17th		C/78 returned to rest billets at HAMEL	
	18th to 22nd		Brigade carried out skeleton drill order & ingase manoeuvre, battery races, laying examinations, N.C.O.'s compass rise & signalling.	
	23rd		Half the horses of the Bde were mallened for glanders – no reaction occurred. Saint R.O. Warden A/78 was acarsted with D.S.O. by II Army Commander.	
"	24th		Batteries carried out gun drill, laying & signalling	
	25th		Rest of the horses of the Bde. were mallened – no reaction was suspected	

Army Form C. 2118

WAR DIARY
or
INTELLIGENCE SUMMARY

(Erase heading not required.)

January 1916

Place	Date	Hour	Summary of Events and Information	Remarks and references to Appendices
AUDENFORT	26th		Brigade & battery drill	
	27th		"	
	28th		"	
	29th		Brevet Col E.H.Willis R.A.A appointed Tempy Brig General & posted to 12th Div.	
	30th		Col E.S. Cleeve R.A posted to 78th Bde R.F.A	
	31st		Battery drill & drain	

Cleeve Col
Commanding 78th Bde R.F.A

78 Br. Ader. R. Ph.
Vol: 8

Army Form C. 2118

WAR DIARY
or
INTELLIGENCE SUMMARY

(Erase heading not required.)

February 1916

Place	Date	Hour	Summary of Events and Information	Remarks and references to Appendices
AUDENFORT	1st to 5th		78th Bde in near training at AUDENFORT, AUDREHEM, HAMEL & CLERQUES	
	6th	8.15 am	The Bde marched via BONNINGUES, NORDAUSQUES, WATTEN to BUYSSCHEURE, arriving in billets at 3 p.m.	
BUYSSCHEURE	7th	9.15 am	The Bde marched via BAVINCHOVE, OXELAERE, CASSEL to STEENVOORDE, arriving in billets at 3 p.m.	
STEENVOORDE	8th		Relief of 40th Bde R.F.A. by 78th Bde R.F.A. commenced. First section of 78th marched via DICKEBUSCH & relieved first section of batteries of 40th Bde in action near KRUISTRAAT on night of 8/9th.	
YPRES	9th		Second section of 78th Bde marched via POPERINGHE to 40th Bde wagon lines & relieved remaining sections of 40th Bde on night of 9/10th. 78th Bde Am. Col. marched via GODEWAERSVELDE & relieved 40th Bde Am. Col. near BOESCHEPE. At 1 p.m. relief of 40th Bde by 78th Bde completed. 78th Bde took over the line from YPRES-COMINES canal to a point 200 yds S.W. of YPRES-COMINES railway covering Trenches 29-37 inclusive, becoming the Left Group of 17th Div Art. D/81 attached to Left Group for all tactical purposes.	
"	10th	3 p.m. 3.45 p.m.	C Battery heavily shelled by the enemy - no damage done. Enemy heavily shelled Trenches 29 to 37; Bde retaliated.	

Army Form C. 2118

WAR DIARY
or
INTELLIGENCE SUMMARY

(Erase heading not required.)

February 1916

Instructions regarding War Diaries and Intelligence Summaries are contained in F. S. Regs., Part II. and the Staff Manual respectively. Title Pages will be prepared in manuscript.

Place	Date	Hour	Summary of Events and Information	Remarks and references to Appendices
YPRES	11th	3 p.m.	Our trenches 31 to 37 were heavily shelled by the enemy. The Group retaliated.	
"	12th	2.30 pm	Enemy shelled our trenches & gun positions. Left group retaliated. Major J. Lindsay Henderson commanding D Battery evacuated sick.	
"	13th		Quiet day	
"	14th	3 p.m.	Enemy shelling very heavily our trenches 29.15.37. Formed an intense barrage behind Reserve Work & Battalion HQ. Left Group retaliated in conjunction with H.A.R. Group again retaliated	
		4.05 pm		
		4.10 pm	" " "	
		4.23 pm	" " "	
		4.31 pm	" " "	
		5.28 pm	" " "	
		6.20 pm	" " "	
			At 5.30 p.m. all communication with front between Infantry & Artillery. At 6.30 p.m. was a more men were blown up by the enemy who then attacked + occupied	
		6.30 pm	our front line trenches from 29 - 33 inclusive & also the BLUFF. C Battery & left section of B Battery were shelled out of their positions from 6.30 p.m. to 6.30 a.m. Left Group barraged on enemy front line + support trenches at varying rates of fire.	
		11.30 pm	Supported Counter attack with rapid fire.	
	15th	4 a.m.	Again supported Counter attack with assistance of 2nd NORTHUMBRIAN Bde. R.F.A on the left.	

1875 W:. W593/826 1,000,000 4/15 J.B.C. & A. A.D.S.S./Forms/C.2118.

Army Form C. 2118

WAR DIARY
or
INTELLIGENCE SUMMARY
(Erase heading not required.)

February 1916

(25)

Place	Date	Hour	Summary of Events and Information	Remarks and references to Appendices
YPRES	15th	5 a.m	4 guns temporarily out of action this morning limbers. 5036 rounds fired since 12 noon 14th.	
	"	6 p.m.	Batteries fired occasional rounds onto enemy old front line.	
	"	8 p.m	Left group bombard whole of enemy old front line in conjunction with H.A.R.	
	"	9 p.m	Infantry counter attacked	
	"	11 p.m	Batteries slackened fire	
	16th	8 p.m	Group opened fire & banged at slow rate of fire enemy trenches 34 to Bluff until 4:30 a.m	
		5:35 a.m 16	An intense barrage was formed & fire ceased at 6 a.m.	
"	17th	5:40 a.m	St. 9 C. slowly RFA of D battery killed	
"	18th		Quiet morning. At 4 p.m. bombard enemy old front line support trench in conjunction with H.A.R. Enemy retaliated heavily and attempted an attack which drove down our own artillery & machine gun fire. Left Group banged enemy old front line from Trench 30 to 33 from 8.45 p.m to 6 a.m at slow rate of fire.	
"	19th			

Army Form C. 2118

WAR DIARY
or
INTELLIGENCE SUMMARY

(Erase heading not required.)

February 1916

Instructions regarding War Diaries and Intelligence Summaries are contained in F. S. Regs., Part II. and the Staff Manual respectively. Title Pages will be prepared in manuscript.

Place	Date	Hour	Summary of Events and Information	Remarks and references to Appendices
YPRES	19th.		Batteries occupied in registration & verification of lines of fire. D Battery heavily shelled at 3 p.m. Operation became untenable; no damage done. Enemy shelled heavily the area between KRUISTRAAT & DICKEBUSCH	(26
	20th		Batteries continued to registrate their lines. Hostile aircraft very active	
	21st		From 5.00 to 5.05 p.m. & again from 5.30 to 5.35 p.m. bombarded enemy's support trenches in conjunction with H.A.R.	
	22nd.		From 6.00 to 6.05 & again from 6.15 to 6.20 p.m. bombarded enemy's support trenches in conjunction with H.A.R. B/81 shelled enemy's present role front line from 29-32 inclusive during the day. Enemy retaliated on our road & trench tram way	
		3 p.m.	Heavy bombardment heard N.E of YPRES. Lieut. D.A. Nicholls R.F.A. joined 78th Bde & was posted to D/78.	

1875 W. W593/826 1,000,000 4/15 J.B.C. & A. A.D.S.S./Forms/C. 2118.

WAR DIARY or INTELLIGENCE SUMMARY

Army Form C. 2118

(27)

February 1916

Place	Date	Hour	Summary of Events and Information	Remarks and references to Appendices
YPRES	23rd	4.30 a.m.	Casualties from ST ELOI reported that enemy were about to attack at dawn. Left group stood to arms. Shelled enemy's old front-line support trenches from 4.30 a.m. to 4.55 a.m. - nothing happened. B/81 shelled enemy's present role a front-line during the day. D Battery 108th Bde. 24th DIV. came into action on night of 23/24th. under Tactical Command of C.O. Left Group 17th DIV.	
	24th		Bombarded enemy's present role a front-line, support trenches BLUFF from 5.30 - 5.50 p.m. in conjunction with H.A.R. B/81 continued to carry out programme of enfilading enemy's old new front line about trenches 30, 31 - 32. One section of 23rd Battery came into action on night of 24/25th under Tactical command of C.O. Left Group. D Battery 106th Bde 24 DIV came into action night of 24/25th were place under Tactical command of C.O. Left Group.	

Army Form C. 2118

WAR DIARY
or
INTELLIGENCE SUMMARY
(Erase heading not required.)

Instructions regarding War Diaries and Intelligence Summaries are contained in F.S. Regs., Part II. and the Staff Manual respectively. Title Pages will be prepared in manuscript.

February 1916

Place	Date	Hour	Summary of Events and Information	Remarks and references to Appendices
YPRES	25th	10 a.m.	Group retaliated opposite trenches 30 + 31 on request of Infantry from 6.00 to 6.05 p.m. & again from 6.20 to 6.25 p.m. Group bombarded enemy's sea front line support trenches in conjunction with H.A.R. B/81 continued to deal with sting points in enemy's front sea front line about trenches 30 & 33. C Battery 104th Bde. R.F.A. came into action night 25/26 two places under tactical command of C.O. Left Group.	
	26th	5.30 a.m.	Bombarded enemy's sea front line from 5.30 – 5.45 a.m. from 5.10 to 5.20 p.m. Bombarded enemy's trenches. Enemy retaliated heavily opening heavy rifle fire thro' grenades evidently expecting an attack.	
	27th		Bombarded enemy's sea front line for 10 mins at dawn. From 5.35 to 5.45 p.m. Bombarded enemy's trenches in conjunction with H.A.R.	
	28th		Carried out bombardments from 6.00 a.m. to 6.15 a.m. together with H.A.R. B/81. continued to shell enemy's sea & front line during the day.	

WAR DIARY or INTELLIGENCE SUMMARY

Army Form C. 2118

February 1916

Place	Date	Hour	Summary of Events and Information	Remarks and references to Appendices
YPRES	28th.		Capt. O.M. Lund R.F.A. joined the 15th Bde. & was posted to command D Battery	
	29th.		Barraged enemy support trenches from 5.10 to 5.20 p.m. when H.A.R. shelled the trenches retiring points.	

Reeve Colonel
Comdg. 15th Bde. RFA.

URFA 78 RFA Vol 9

Army Form C. 2118

WAR DIARY
or
INTELLIGENCE SUMMARY

(Erase heading not required.)

March 1916

29

Instructions regarding War Diaries and Intelligence Summaries are contained in F. S. Regs., Part II. and the Staff Manual respectively. Title Pages will be prepared in manuscript.

Place	Date	Hour	Summary of Events and Information	Remarks and references to Appendices
YPRES	1	12 noon	Five 18pdrs of 2nd E"R"d Battery of 2nd NORTHUMBRIAN Bde & 2 4·5" Hows of D/61 placed under Tactical Command of O.C. 78th Bde. commanding Left group.	Ref. 15 2nd Army Trench Maps 1/10000 Sheet N°7 HOLLEBEKE
		5:15 pm	Left group opened fire & barraged along the line of enemy's support trench I34b62 - 41 - d27 - 24 - 03 - d01 - 04a88 with 26 guns as follows 78 Bde 14 18pdrs. 23rd Battery 2 18pdrs 24 Div 8 18pdrs	
		5:20 pm	All guns lifted to I34b92 - d19 - 67 - 44 - 20 - 04b 27 & continued a barrage till 5·45 p.m.	
		5:25 pm	when are fire ceased. Rate of fire was action fire 10 secs. Enemy did not retaliate. Much damage done to enemy's trenches	
	2	4:30 am	Three battalions of 76th Bde assaulted the BLUFF + trenches 29 to 33 inclusive which were taken by the enemy on the 14th February.	
		4:32 am	The artillery opened fire & Left group consisting of A, B, C, D/78, D/106, C/107, D/106 + 23rd Battery + the How Battery D/81 opened fire simultaneously with the Heavy artillery forming a barrage along the line of enemy's support trenches I34b92 - d19 - 67 - 44 - 20 - 04b 27. D/108 fired in enfilade along the same line. The 5 18pdrs of 2nd Northumbrian Bde RFA + the 2 Hows. of D/61 of 50th. Div created a barrage along the line I34b90 - d82 9 sup 64 including the road I35 c 06. The rate of fire was action fire 10 secs for 1st half hour " 15 " 2nd " " " 20 " then then onwards.	

WAR DIARY

Army Form C. 2118

30

March 1916

Place	Date	Hour	Summary of Events and Information	Remarks and references to Appendices
YPRES	2	6 a.m.	About this time fire was slowly reduced & the barrage maintained during the rear of the day at a slower rate with occasional bursts of rapid fire. The Infantry assault was successful & the BLUFF & lost trenches retaken & also about 100 yds. of the original German front line known as the BEAN. The enemy retaliated with a heavy bombardment with 4.2", 5.9" & 8" Guns & Howitzers on our support & communication trenches during the whole of the day & night of the 2nd. During the action A, B, & D Battery 78th Bde supplied one officer with each assaulting battalion who acted as F.O.O. & liaison officer to the Battalion Commander. One officer from 78th Bde R.F.A. Head Qrs. was also attached to the Brig. Gen. Commanding & liaison officer. All communication lines down except between Inf. Bde H.Q. & Left Group. H.Q. but messages were never sent again from F.O.O's.	
			From 12 noon on the 1st to 12 noon on the 2nd the Left Group fired 15588 rds. C/75 firing in the 4th column 2902 rds. Casualties with Left Group Artillery were: 1 officer wounded, 6 men killed & 4 men wounded. The wounded officer was Lieut. D.A. Nicolls of D/75. Two guns of the Group were temporarily out of action with broken springs.	

WAR DIARY
INTELLIGENCE SUMMARY

(Erase heading not required.)

Army Form C. 2118

March 1916

Place	Date	Hour	Summary of Events and Information	Remarks and references to Appendices
YPRES	3		Several of the guns became so hot that they had to be covered with water. About 25% H.E. was fired by the 18 pdrs. Enemy artillery was very active during the whole of the day & night	
	4	11 a.m.	On the enemy continuing to shell our trenches intermittently A.B.C & D batteries were ranged on fire 2 mins rapid, 2 mins pause & 2 mins repeat every 1½ hours on the barrage line I34 r 9.2 – O 16 27	
		4:30 p.m. 16 5:30 p.m.	Enemy heavily shelled dug outs near Bde H Q at H 2 4 a 2 5 (Sheet 28 NW 1/20000) & also around battery positions. D/76 heavily shelled by 5.9" & 4.2" – 5 casualties – no other damage excepting to fifteen men	
		9 p.m.	all quiet	
	5		Infantry & regular artillery not active as on rest & renew enemy fire. Quiet day	

WAR DIARY
INTELLIGENCE SUMMARY
(Erase heading not required.)

Army Form C. 2118

32

Place	Date	Hour	Summary of Events and Information	Remarks and references to Appendices
YPRES	6	9 a.m.	Army quiet night	
		3 p.m.	Enemy shelled KRUISTRAAT slightly	
	7	10.45 a.m.	Army Commander inspected representative body of men from 76th Bde. R.F.A & thanked them for the good work done during the operations of March 1, 2nd & 3rd.	
			Quiet day; much snow	
	8		Quiet day on Left Group front	
		6 p.m.	Some hostile fire around KRUISTRAAT. Wames of probable attack from direction of HILL 60	
			Orders received for relief of 76th Bde R.F.A by 40th Bde R.F.A	
	9	1 p.m.	Quiet night, much snow (3") very cold	
			Relief of 17 Div Art by 3rd Div Art commenced. D/76th relieved by 23rd Bty.	
	10	9 a.m.	D/76 marched to rest billets at CAESTRE	

Army Form C. 2118

WAR DIARY
INTELLIGENCE SUMMARY

(Erase heading not required.)

March 1916

No. 33

Place	Date	Hour	Summary of Events and Information	Remarks and references to Appendices
YPRES	10	2.45 pm	Infantry warn artillery of suspected mine near Trenches 32 & 33	
"	11	9.15	That relieving section of A.B.C. Btys march to rest area near CAESTRE	
		6 pm	Gun relieving personnel of A/78 relieved by 6th Bty, B/78 by 49th Bty, C/78 by 49th Bty. Relieved personnel of 78th Bde to rest area by motor bus	
"	12th	9.15	Second relieving sections of A.B.C. Btys march to CAESTRE	
		12 noon	78th Bde H.Q. relieved by 40th Bde R.F.A. at 12 noon. 78th Bde H.Q. march to rest area	
		6 pm	Personnel of second relieving sections of A.B.C. Batteries to rest area by motor bus	
CAESTRE	13		Bde in rest at CAESTRE	
"	14		idem	
"	15		Orders received & issued for the relief of 31st Div DIV by 17th DIV.	
"	16		Battery Commanders & adjutant proceed to ARMENTIERES to reconnoitre & arrange details of relief of 31st DIV. A.T.	

WAR DIARY
or
INTELLIGENCE SUMMARY

Army Form C. 2118

March 1916

Place	Date	Hour	Summary of Events and Information	Remarks and references to Appendices
CAESTRE	17		Advance parties of B + D/78 proceeded to ARMENTIERE. 2/st S Stradion joined the Bde Hqtrs to B/78.	
	18	9.30am	First relieving section of B/78 + D/78 marched to 21st Div. area via BAILLEUL + NIEPPE & relieved sections of B + D/94 Bde. RFA	
	19	9.30am	Second relieving section of B/78 + D/78 marched to 21st Div. area & relieved section of B + D/94 Bde RFA	
	20	9am	18th Bde. Am Col. marched to 21st Div. Area & relieved 94th Bde Am Col.	
	21		Advance parties of 10 officers 21 telephonists of A/78 + C/78 marched to A/94 + C/94 2/st S Stradion joined 75th Bde + posted to B/78.	
	22	9.30am	First relieving sections of A/78 + C/78 marched to 21st Div area & relieved first sections of A/94 + C/94	
	23	9.30	Second sections of A/78 + C/78 marched to 21st Div Area relieved second section of A/94 + C/94	
ARMENTIERES		12 noon	78th Bde HQ relieved 94th Bde HQ RFA.	
	24		Quiet day	

WAR DIARY
or
INTELLIGENCE SUMMARY

(Erase heading not required.)

Army Form C. 2118

35

March 1916

Place	Date	Hour	Summary of Events and Information	Remarks and references to Appendices
ARMENTIERES	25	—		
	26	—		
	27		Heavy firing north from 4 a.m to 6 a.m	
	28	—		
	29	—		
	30		Left section of B/76 shelled by 5.9" How. from 9.30 am to 1.05 pm with about 100 ms. Position badly knocked about & one gun damaged. 2/Lieuts H.W Taylor joined the Bde & posted to A/76 + D/76 respectively. W.S. MacLean. 6 officers & 90 men of 2nd Australian Div attached to 76th Bde R.F.A. for instruction. B/76 + D/76 carried out retaliations on enemy trenches opposite T 60 & 61	

Reeve Col
C/76 Bde RFA

Vol 10
78 RFA
36
XV ⁴

Army Form C. 2118

WAR DIARY
or
INTELLIGENCE SUMMARY
(Erase heading not required.)

Instructions regarding War Diaries and Intelligence Summaries are contained in F.S. Regs., Part II. and the Staff Manual respectively. Title Pages will be prepared in manuscript.

APRIL 1916

Place	Date	Hour	Summary of Events and Information	Remarks and references to Appendices
ARMENTIERES	1	9.30 am	Enemy heavily shelled the Dirage & near C/78's Battery Position. One Australian Sergt who was attached to this Battery for instruction was killed. There were no other casualties. B/78's had two horses wounded in their wagon line from splinters from shelling of Heavy Gun at B17b (Sheet 36)	Sheet 36 NW
	2	5am	Colonel Reeve left on leave & Colonel Hardman Cmdg the Brigade during his absence. B/78'n had two horses wounded by splinters from the shelling of a Heavy Battery at C13c (sheet 36)	
	3		All quiet on our front.	
	4		B/78'n moved their wagon line to B9.d.S.1	Sheet 36 N.W.
	5		All quiet on our front	
	6		The enemy fired a large number of small shells 7.7 cm into various points in our zone. No damage was done.	
	7		All quiet on our front. C/81 engaged a snipers post at C29.c.5.8 with apparently good results	

Army Form C. 2118

37

WAR DIARY
or
INTELLIGENCE SUMMARY
(Erase heading not required.)

APRIL 1916

Instructions regarding War Diaries and Intelligence Summaries are contained in F. S. Regs., Part II. and the Staff Manual respectively. Title Pages will be prepared in manuscript.

Place	Date	Hour	Summary of Events and Information	Remarks and references to Appendices
ARMENTIERES	8		Quiet day.	
	9		" "	
	10		" "	
	11		" "	
	12		Very quiet day. Lt Ridout posted to the 81st Bn sigde Ammn Column. Capt R. Joce appointed Adjt of the 7th & 8th Bgde R.F.A.	
	13		Very quiet day	
	14		—	
	15		—	
	16		Quiet day.	
	17		Quiet day. 2nd Lt W. of Provid) No 3. T.F. Arty Training School, attached 2nd Lt W. a. Rees) to A + D Btys for introduction	
	18		Cloudy & rain. Quiet day.	
	19		—	
	20	8.45 a.m	Enemy heavily shelled trenches 74 and 75. Enemy French mortars were also used in the bombardment. Part of an aerial torpedo was picked up & sent to C.I.R.A. A fair amount of damage was done to our trenches, but no lives were lost.	

Army Form C. 2118

WAR DIARY
or
INTELLIGENCE SUMMARY
(Erase heading not required.)

APRIL 1916

38

Place	Date	Hour	Summary of Events and Information	Remarks and references to Appendices
ARMENTIERES	21		Quiet day.	
		4. P.M.	Retaliated for enemy shelling of the 20th by continued bombardment of his trenches. A, B and C Batteries fired 40 rounds each H.E on enemy works and trenches A/78th I 5 d 3.6 to 2.5 B/78th I 5 a 5.5 to I.12 a.5.5 C/76th B/81? I 5 b 2.1.5 to 3.3 I 5 b 4.1 to I 5 d 3.7½ The 6" Howrs also fired behind the enemy's front line. Small retaliation	Sheet 36 N.W. 1/20,000
	22		All quiet	
	23		All quiet	
	24		Enemy heavily bombarded our front and support trenches in the region of Port Ballot & l'Epinette. About 500 shells of various calibre were distributed along this front. Very small damage was done.	
	25		A quiet day.	

WAR DIARY or INTELLIGENCE SUMMARY

APRIL 1916

Army Form C. 2118

Place	Date	Hour	Summary of Events and Information	Remarks and references to Appendices
ARMENTIERES	26	3 PM to 3.30 PM	Bombarded the enemy's front line in the region of Port Mullet Salient in retaliation for his shelling of the 24th. The 6" How. fired 90 rounds on his front line & the 4.5" & French mortars & 18 pdrs also took part. A fair amount of damage was done to his trenches. There was small retaliation.	
	27		Quiet day.	
	28		Quiet day. 2nd Lt. A.J. Dainty and 2nd Lt. L.G.L. Alder joined 7 Brigade & were posted to the Bogie Amm Column.	
	29		Quiet day	
	30			

Pleene Colonel
Comdg 7 Bde RFA

XVII 78 RFA
Army Form C. 2118
VOL 1140

WAR DIARY
or
INTELLIGENCE SUMMARY
(Erase heading not required.)

MAY 1916

Place	Date	Hour	Summary of Events and Information	Remarks and references to Appendices
ARMENTIERES	1.		Quiet day.	
	2.	1 P.M.	Enemy shelled our trenches of L'EPINETTE salient. All Batteries retaliated with 24 rounds per Battery.	
		1.30 PM.	Enemy again shelled our trenches of L'EPINETTE salient. We retaliated with A.C. & B/81st with 24 rounds per battery.	
		2.PM.	All reported quiet.	
	3.		Fine sunny day; all quiet.	
	4.		Fine day; all quiet	
	5.	10 a.m.	O.C. of N.Z. Art (Col Symon) visited Brigade & was shown Battery positions etc by O.C. 78th	
		6.30 PM.	Enemy shelled trenches of L'EPINETTE salient heavily. Bde fired retaliation "A" force. This was not sufficient & Batteries continued to retaliate independently in accordance with Infantry request. Several gas alarms were sounded, but these were due to gas shells, there being a N'westerly wind. All reported quiet about 9.30 PM. Two Officers with the Bde for instruction, 2nd Lt BOND and 2nd Lt W.G. A.REES left for return to ENGLAND.	
	6.		Quiet day; 2nd Lt DAVIS of N.Z. Div attached to C/78th	

WAR DIARY or INTELLIGENCE SUMMARY

Army Form C. 2118

MAY 1916

Place	Date	Hour	Summary of Events and Information	Remarks and references to Appendices
ARMENTIERES	7		Quiet day	
	8		Infantry reported searchlight troublesome, location near FUNGHEREAU or L' AVENTURE. A. C & B/81st and battery of 6" Hows received orders to fire on & if possible destroy same, shewed it appeared. In searchlight appeared.	SHEET 36 N.W.
	9		5 Bty Commdrs & 4 Subalterns, the Adjt & 50 other ranks of the N.Z. Div arrived & proceeded to the Batteries they would ultimately relieve.	
	10		Quiet day	
	11	8.30 am	Trenches 79 & 80 shelled. We retaliated on trenches opposite. B Bty with 27 rounds & B/81st with 45 rounds. Later all quiet.	
	12	4.30 pm	Trenches 79 & 80 heavily shelled by enemy 4.2. B/75th & B/81st retaliated. Later all reported quiet.	
	13		Quiet day	
	14		Quiet day	
	15		Quiet day	
	16		Quiet day	
	17		Batteries of Bgde relieved by Batteries of 1st Bgde N.Z. F.A. Relief completed by 12 noon on the 17th. "A" relieved by 1st Bty, "B" by 3rd Bty, "C" by 8 & 9 Bty, "D" by 7 Bty, & B/81st by 15th How Bty.	

Army Form C. 2118

WAR DIARY
or
INTELLIGENCE SUMMARY
(Erase heading not required.)

42.

Place	Date	Hour	Summary of Events and Information	Remarks and references to Appendices
	18.		Regt. marched to Billets at VIEUX BERQUIN arriving at 1 a.m. Bgde marched to Billets at RENESCURE arriving at 6 P.M.	SHEET 36a.
VIEUX BERQUIN	19.		Bgde marched to rest area. Regt. H.Q. BAYENGHEM A & B Btys "A"&"B" BAYENGHEM. "C" Bty AFFRINGUES. "D" Bty "SENINGHEM. D/78 - (O.C. Capt LUND) left B/81st LA RT. Joins 78. Bgde as D/78. B Bde as A/81st . B/81st (O.C. Major SUTTON) Battery training	5 = HAZEBROUCK
BAYENGHEM LEZ SENINGHEM	27.		Regt. Drill order	SHEET 27a S.E.
	29		Regt. Drill Order. Divisional day in training area.	
	30		Battery training	
	31		" "	

Rhodes - Col.
Comdg 78th Bde. R.F.A.

June

78 RFA
4550 12

Army Form C. 2118

WAR DIARY
or
INTELLIGENCE SUMMARY

XVy

(Erase heading not required.)

JUNE 1916

Place	Date	Hour	Summary of Events and Information	Remarks and references to Appendices
BAYENGHEM LEZ SENINGHEM	1st to 9th		Brigade in training	
	10		Brigade marched from BAYENGHEM lez SENINGHEM to THEROUANNE	5/a HAZEBROUCK
	11		Brigade left THEROUANNE and marched to HENRICOURT	"
	12		Brigade left HENRICOURT and marched to Bouque MAISON	"
	13		" " Bouque MAISON and marched to TALMAS and joined 4th ARMY.	SHEET 62°/40000
	14		" " TALMAS and marched to HEILLY.	"
	15		" " HEILLY and marched to VILLE SUR ANCRE	"
	20		Col. S. 3.3. CLEEVE promoted Brig General and posted to 6th DIV as C.R.A.	
	21		Lt Col R St George KIRKE assumed command of the Brigade vice Brig General Cleeve	
	23		Brigade came into action E24a	SHEET 62ª
	30		Bombarded continuously night and day enemy lines & defences FRICOURT and retaliations	" 62°

J Gerald Ns
Lt Col
Commanding 78th Bde R.F.A.

17th Div.
XV. Corps.

WAR DIARY

Headquarters,

78th BRIGADE, R.F.A.

J U L Y

1 9 1 6

Army Form C. 2118

WAR DIARY
or
INTELLIGENCE SUMMARY

(Erase heading not required.)

JULY 1916

Instructions regarding War Diaries and Intelligence Summaries are contained in F. S. Regs., Part II and the Staff Manual respectively. Title Pages will be prepared in manuscript.

Place	Date	Hour	Summary of Events and Information	Remarks and references to Appendices
FRICOURT.	1	6.25 a.m.	The 78th Bde in action in front of FRICOURT & attached to 21st Div Arty less D/78th attached to XV Corps H.A. & B/19 - attached to 78th Bde R.F.A. B & C Batteries each had one section of A/76th attached. Bde was occupied in cutting from F9b.3.8 to F3e.6.9. B/19th was occupied in destruction of strong points in FRICOURT & FRICOURT WOOD.	MONTAUBAN 1/20,000
		7.30 a.m.	Infantry attached N&S of FRICOURT & Bde barraged in rear of village & North of WOOD.	
	2		Bde established slow barrage on FRICOURT WOOD. S.W. of road running from F3.b.9.8. to F3.a.8.4	"
	3		A & C Btys moved forward to F9.a. & continued Barrage Quadrangle Trench.	"
	4		B Bty moved forward to F9.a. Slow barrage was continued on Quadrangle Trench.	"
	5	12.15 am to 12.45 am	Concentrated bombardment of Quadrangle Trench from X23c.2.7 to X22d.7.8 D/19th bombarded from X23c.2.7 to X22d.8.5	"
		12.45 am	Infantry attacked & Bde lifted fire to Quadrangle Support X23b.0.3 to X23a.7.7. D/19th South of Contalmaison. During the following day & night the Bde was occupied in searching BAILIFF WOOD and CONTALMAISON VILLAGE. B Bty moved forward to FRICOURT in F3.a. and C Bty moved forward to F4.c. Bde H.Q moved forward from E24.b. to F9.c.	"

1875. Wt. W593/826 1,000,000 4/15 I.B.C. & A. A.D.S.S./Forms/C. 2118.

Army Form C. 2118

WAR DIARY
or
INTELLIGENCE SUMMARY
(Erase heading not required.)

JULY 1916

Place	Date	Hour	Summary of Events and Information	Remarks and references to Appendices
FRICOURT	6		Bombarded with short concentrated bombardments WOOD TRENCH and WOOD SUPPORT. When not bombarding Pode was occupied in barraging WOOD SUPPORT + QUADRANGLE SUPPORT.	MONTAUBAN 1/20,000
	7		Bombarded Quadrangle Support	
		2 am	Infantry attacked Quadrange Support + Pode lifted to "cutting" NORTH of CONTALMAISON, sweeping roadway East + West of CUTTING	
		6 am	Infantry attack continued successfully + Contalmaison + N.W corner of MAMETZ WOOD was captured.	
	8		Barraged enemys second line	
	9		Barraged enemy's second line + searched VILLA WOOD, MIDDLE WOOD LOWER WOOD + N.W side of MAMETZ WOOD.	
	10		Bombarded WOOD SUPPORT and QUADRANGLE SUPPORT + N.W. edge of MAMETZ WOOD. Infantry attacked Quadrangle support in the early morning with partial success.	

Army Form C. 2118

WAR DIARY
or
INTELLIGENCE SUMMARY
(Erase heading not required.)

JULY 1916

Instructions regarding War Diaries and Intelligence Summaries are contained in F. S. Regs., Part II. and the Staff Manual respectively. Title Pages will be prepared in manuscript.

Place	Date	Hour	Summary of Events and Information	Remarks and references to Appendices
FRICOURT.	11.		Barraged N. Edge of Mametz Wood & Lower Wood. Infantry captured whole of Mametz Wood & Lower Wood & Pearl Alley. Bde lifted to CONTALMAISON VILLA & enemy's second line, which was continually kept under fire.	MARTIN PUICH ½ 20,000
	12.		Bde kept under continual fire BAZENTIN LE PETIT WOOD & VILLAGE & enemy's second line	"
	13.		ditto	
	14.	3.20 a.m. to 3.25 a.m.	Intense bombardment of enemy's second line. Bde then lifted to BAZENTIN LE PETIT in one lift & continued to barrage N. of BAZENTIN LE PETIT throughout the day & at night searched road running through S.14 & S.2.a. Infantry attack successful both Wood & Village being captured	"
	15.		Maintained a slow barrage on roads north of BAZENTIN LE PETIT	
	16.		Bde kept Switch Trench & Martinpuich under continual fire. One section of B. & C. Batteries advanced to Valley on E side of Mametz Wood & took up positions near FLATIRON COPSE	"
	17.		Bde kept switch Trench & Martinpuich under continual fire, with bursts of fire into High Wood B/175" moved advanced section back about 500yds owing to Heavy [illegible] fire.	

Army Form C. 2118

WAR DIARY
or
INTELLIGENCE SUMMARY
(Erase heading not required.)

JULY. 1916

47.

Instructions regarding War Diaries and Intelligence Summaries are contained in F. S. Regs., Part II. and the Staff Manual respectively. Title Pages will be prepared in manuscript.

Place	Date	Hour	Summary of Events and Information	Remarks and references to Appendices
FRICOURT	18		Bde. covered zone for defence from Railway in S.2.c.0.8 to S.2.a.8.1 and one Section of B/76th shelled MARTINPUICH in M.32 a+c. C/76th moved the whole battery forward to the W of MAMETZ WOOD & occupied a position in x.17.d.	MARTINPUICH 1/20,000
	19.		Kept Switch Trench & High Wood under continual fire. Bombarded High Wood during the night	
	20		Pounded during day & night from S.2.c.0.8 to S.2.a.8.1 with occasional bursts of fire in MARTINPUICH.	
	21	3.20am & 5.30am	Concentrated bombardment of Switch Trench from S.2.b.6.6 to S.2.c.0.8	
	22.	7pm & 12.30am	Bombarded Switch Trench from M.33.d.3.1. to M.33.d.0.2 Infantry attack successful H.Q. 78th Bde moved from F.9.c to F.4.c.	
	23		78th Bde relieved by the 25th Bde R.F.A. D/78th rejoined the 78th Bde R.F.A.	
		11PM	Batteries marched to DERNANCOURT	FRANCE SHEET 62D 1/40,000
	24		Bde in rest at DERNANCOURT.	

Army Form C. 2118

WAR DIARY
or
INTELLIGENCE SUMMARY
(Erase heading not required.)

JULY 1916

Place	Date	Hour	Summary of Events and Information	Remarks and references to Appendices
DERNACOURT	25 to 31		Bde in rest.	

When Batteries advanced they were unable to find any emplacements for guns, until last position was occupied, when splinter proof covering was found. Gun guns.
Visual signalling was found to be effective. Lamp signalling proved the best.

Casualties in men Wounded 21
                    Killed 5.

Casualties in Horses from shell fire 11
As Mobile Vet Section   18.

Total number of rounds fired during operations

	A	Ax
A/78ᵗʰ	15433	7542
B/78ᵗʰ	15099	7645
C/78ᵗʰ	15798	7441
B/79ᵗʰ	6152	

Total number of rounds fired 75,080.

J. Gleed Lt. Col.
Comdg 78ᵗʰ Bde R.F.A.

17th Divisional Artillery.

78th BRIGADE

ROYAL FIELD ARTILLERY.

AUGUST 1 9 1 6 ::::::

Ammunition expenditure.
Casualties.

WAR DIARY
INTELLIGENCE SUMMARY

78 Bde RFA 49.

AUGUST 1916

Place	Date	Hour	Summary of Events and Information	Remarks and references to Appendices
DERNAN-COURT	1	—	The 78th Bde was at DERNANCOURT.	
		6 p.m.	The Brigade relieved the 162 Bde RFA of 33rd Div in the line in front of LONGEVAL & took up the following positions HQ S21d86 A S21d59 (6 guns) C S21d68 (6 guns) D S20a73	Map. 5TCSW
MONTAUBAN	2		Two guns of B were attached to A & C batteries which were armed lately as 6 gun batteries. 3 guns covered war from S11a30 – S11f10 Major F. Sutton DSO commanding D battery detached to command 80R Bde RFA	"
"			All guns carefully registered & calibrated on zone. From 5:30 pm to 7 pm bombarded enemy front line from S11a11 – S11c77. Rate of fire 1 rd per gun per 2 minutes. Enemy shelled battery positions & Bde HQ during the night from 8 pm to 4 a.m. all ground behind enemy front line in Bois one except at a slow rate of fire.	"
"	3		Batteries occupied in cutting wire about strong point (S11c58) Bombarded enemy front line from 5:30 pm to 7 pm & repeated at 8:10 pm as on the 2nd August.	"

Army Form C. 2118

WAR DIARY
INTELLIGENCE SUMMARY
(Erase heading not required.)

AUGUST 1916   **78th Bde R.F.A**   **50**

Place	Date	Hour	Summary of Events and Information	Remarks and references to Appendices
MONTAUBAN	4	12:35 a.m	Intense bombardment of enemy's front line in S.me. At 12:40 artillery lifted 200 yds and infantry were to have attacked but attack postponed.	Map 57c SW
"	5		Day night firing carried out to prevent work by the enemy & to prevent him bringing up reinforcements + supplies, 18 par. firing 500 rds by day + 625 rds by night + 4.5 How battery 330 rds by day + 166 by night. Battery positions were heavily shelled by enemy. One 4.5 How + one 18 par. put out of action	"
"	6		Usual day + night firing carried out.	"
"	7		From 5:30 – 6:30 p.m. bombarded enemy's front-line S.11.d.5.1. – S.11.d.5.7. 9 ores. per g.un.	
"	8		From 5:30 – 6:30 p.m. bombarded ORCHARD Trench from its junction with DELVILLE WOOD to WOOD LANE (S.12.c.16 – S.12.c.59). Repeated at 7:20 a.m. At 7:40 a.m. fire was lifted 400 yds + continued for 1 hour – infantry attacked successfully.	"
"	9		Ordinary day night firing on back areas carried out.	
"	10		Ordinary day night firing + a desultory barrage N of DELVILLE WOOD maintained for 1 hour at 7:30 p.m.	

Army Form C. 2118

WAR DIARY
or
INTELLIGENCE SUMMARY
(Erase heading not required.) 78th Bde R.F.A.

AUGUST 51

Place	Date	Hour	Summary of Events and Information	Remarks and references to Appendices
MONTAUBAN	11		Day + night firing carried out + desultory barrage N of DELVILLE WOOD maintained for 1 hour at 7.30p.m. 300 yds clear of wood.	Map 57C S.W.
	12		Usual day + night firing carried out + hostile gun positions at M36 b 6 1 + M 36 d 9 1 shelled with bursts of fire at irregular intervals. D Battery shelled FLERS + roads + road junctions from 12 noon to 2p.m. Area of 78th Bde positions shelled by 2.00 4.2's, 5.9's +8.2's	"
	13		Day + night firing carried out and bursts of fire maintained on hostile gun positions. Hostile fire below normal	"
	14		Usual day + night firing	"
	15		"	"
	16		"	"

Army Form C. 2118

WAR DIARY
~~INTELLIGENCE SUMMARY~~
(Erase heading not required.)

AUGUST   78th Bde RFA   52

Place	Date	Hour	Summary of Events and Information	Remarks and references to Appendices
MONTAUBAN	17	8 a.m.	Bombardment commenced of enemy's front line with frequent searching in 3rd line. A Battery occupied in cutting wire on Divisional front. Strong points & dug outs shelled by 4.5" Hows. During the night fire maintained on targets to engage during the day	Map. 57c SW
	18	6 a.m.	Bombardment resumed in all fronts with periods of intense fire on the front line	"
		2:45 pm	(Zeitoun) intense shrapnel barrage in front line + infantry (41st Bde) advanced as far as possible into our barrage. At 2:50 pm barrage lifted 200 yds & infantry successfully assaulted. At 3:00 pm barrage lifted another 200 yds. At 3:30 p.m artillery swept back along communication trenches till 3:30 p.m after which time barrage maintained in front fronts of the ORCHARD Trench successfully captured to its junction with DELVILLE WOOD	"
		At 10. p.m reached ground N E of DELVILLE WOOD with bursts of heavy shrapnel fire till 11:30 p.m.	
	19		Day & night firing carried out at least 400 yds clear of DELVILLE WOOD	

Army Form C. 2118

WAR DIARY
or
INTELLIGENCE SUMMARY
(Erase heading not required.)

78[K] Bde RFA

AUGUST 1916

53

Place	Date	Hour	Summary of Events and Information	Remarks and references to Appendices
MONTAUBAN	20	—	The 78th Bde withdrew from the line between 4 pm & 6 pm & was taken over temporarily by 5th Div Art to be finally taken over by 7th Div Arty. Ammunition, maps, telephone wires were handed over to 14th Bde RFA 7th Div Art Batteries march to BONNAY arriving about 10 p m when bivouacked	
BONNAY	21.		Brigade in rest at BONNAY	
BONNAY			Parade for Corps Commander (XV) at 2.30 pm then returned for work done during month of July & August	
	22		Bde marched at 8.55 a.m. via LANEUVILLE, PONT NOYELLES, QUERRIEU to ALLONVILLE there billeted.	
ALLONVILLE	23		At 9 p.m. Brigade marched via BERTANGLES, FLESSELLES, CANAPLES, MONTRELET, FIENVILLERS to GAUDIEMPRÉ in camp at OCCOCHES	
OCCOCHES	24		Brigade marched to GAUDIEMPRÉ via DOULLENS + POMMERA at 6 a.m.	
GAUDIEMPRE	25		Brigade in rest at GAUDIEMPRE	

Army Form C. 2118

WAR DIARY
or
INTELLIGENCE SUMMARY
(Erase heading not required.)

AUGUST 1916   78th Bde RFA

54

Place	Date	Hour	Summary of Events and Information	Remarks and references to Appendices
GAUDIEMPRE	26		One section of each battery A.B.C. & one gun of D battery relieved corresponding section & gun of 56th Div. Art in Northern group opposite GOMMECOURT	Map. 57D NE
"	27		One 4.5 How retired one 4.5 How of 56th Div Art	
"	28			
"	29		Remaining section of A B C & D batteries relieved corresponding sections of 56th Div. Art in northern group.	
BIENVILLERS	30		78th Bde H.Q. took over Northern group at 10 a.m. Also came under tactical command of O.C. northern group.	
"	31			

J. Grey Kerr
Lt Col
Cmdg 78th Bde RFA

78th Brigade R.F.A.

Ammunition expended from August 1st., to August 20th.

	A.	AX.	BX.	Total.
A/78th -6 guns -	8870	5474	-	14344
C/78th -6 guns -	6352	5518	-	11870
D/78th 4 guns			4083	4083
Total	15222	10992	4083	30297

CASUALTIES - August 1st., to August 20th.

	Officers	O.Ranks.	Total.
Killed	1	4	5
Wounded	2	11	13
Shell Shock	-	9	9
	3	24	27

Officer Killed - Lieut: A.S.Lloyd R.F.A. of "C" Battery.
Officer Wounded - Lieut: H.G.Pincent R.F.A. of "D" Battery.
"   "   - 2/Lieut: R.J.Yeatman R.F.A. of "B" Battery.

78th Brigade R.F.A.

Ammunition expended from August 1st., to August 20th.

	A.	AX.	BX.	Total.
A/78th -6 guns -	8870	5474	-	14344
C/78th -6 guns -	6352	5518	-	11870
D/78th 4 guns			4083	4083
Total	15222	10992	4083	30297

CASUALTIES - August 1st., to August 20th.

	Officers	O.Ranks.	Total.
Killed	1	4	5
Wounded	2	11	13
Shell Shock	-	9	9
	3	24	27

Officer Killed - Lieut: A.S.Lloyd R.F.A. of "C" Battery.

Officer Wounded - Lieut: H.G.Pincent R.F.A. of "D" Battery.

" " - 2/Lieut: R.J.Yeatman R.F.A. of "B" Battery.

WO 15

Army Form C. 2118

WAR DIARY
or
INTELLIGENCE SUMMARY
(Erase heading not required.)

78th Bde. R.F.A.   September 1916   55

Place	Date	Hour	Summary of Events and Information	Remarks and references to Appendices
BIENVILLERS	1		78th Bde. in action W. of MONCHY-AU-BOIS & GOMMECOURT & covering the Zone E.11.q.6 to E.25.c.9, constituting Northern Group. with A/80 Bde. (4 guns) attached. The 78th Bde. reorganised into 3 6 gun batteries, one 4.5 How Bty of 4 guns as follows:- A/78 absorbed 1 section of A/80. Map 57D.N.E.
			B/78 " " " of A/80	
			C/78 " " " of B/80	
	2		One section of reorganised C/78 loaned for tactical purposes to Centre Group under O.C. 81st Bde. R.F.A.	A/F
			The following officers joined the Bde.	
			2/Lt. A.S. MARSH R.F.A.	
			1/Lt. E.P. VERNALL R.F.A.	
			Lt. A.E. HAYNES R.F.A.	
			2/Lt. H. DENHAM-SMITH R.F.A.	
			2/Lt. E. WORTHINGTON-EYRE R.F.A	
	3	8 pm	Gas Alert.	A/F
			Batteries occupied in registration & calibration in zones.	
		F. Sup.	Gas Alert Cancelled	A/F

WAR DIARY
or
INTELLIGENCE SUMMARY

Army Form C. 2118

(Erase heading not required.)

September 1916   78th Bde. RFA   5G

Place	Date	Hour	Summary of Events and Information	Remarks and references to Appendices
BIENVILLERS	4		Situation quiet – some Trench Mortaring of our trenches. How. Bty (D/78) retaliated in supposed position of hostile Trench Mortar	Map 57 D. N.E.
	5	6.45 a.m.		
		8.30 p.m.	Gas liberated in Divisional Front. At 8.33 pm to 9.00 pm A B & C batteries shelled GOMMECOURT WOOD tracks & communication trenches E of vital supposed enemy battery positions. Enemy retaliated very slightly. Off wind retaliation & fire on working parties, situation generally very quiet	
	6		"	
	7			
	8		Some Trench Mortaring by the enemy. Group retaliated on lll "Z" E23d42 with 100 rds. H.E. effectively	
	9			
	10		Registration of	
	11		A battery moved one gun forward to E10a to cut a lane in enemy's wire at E11b 33. This was done during the 11th. A front lane was cut about 20 × broad.	

1875 Wt. W593/826 1,000,000 4/15 J.B.C. & A. A.D.S.S./Forms/C. 2118.

WAR DIARY or INTELLIGENCE SUMMARY

Army Form C. 2118

78th Bde. R.F.A.

September 1916.

57.

Place	Date	Hour	Summary of Events and Information	Remarks and references to Appendices
	12		Wire cutting continued by A battery forward gun.	
	13	From 9.30 p.m. to 12 midnight all batteries fired at slow rate of fire to cover more men by heavy calcareous bringing heavy gun into action near HEBUTERNE		
	14		A quiet day, a few T.T. men in trenches in NORTHERN GROUP.	
	15		A & C Batteries were occupied in wire cutting at three points in Group front. Rapid of 20° to 25° cut. The position of forward gun of A Battery was spotted by the enemy + they were shelling with 77's + 4.2 - discharge of gun personnel. A B & C Batteries occurred in wire cutting.	
	16		A B & C Batteries occurred in wire cutting up to 12 noon when forward gun was withdrawn. 20 guns of 32nd Div. Art came into action in Northern Group Area its reserve position were affiliated to Northern Group temporarily.	
	17		Quiet day — a few T.T. mm. shrapnel fires about A/78 — three men wounded. Batteries busy preparing new positions in J.12 + K.8	Map. 57D NE

WAR DIARY
or
INTELLIGENCE SUMMARY

(Erase heading not required.)

Army Form C. 2118

Place: 78th Bde RFA
Date: September 1916

Date	Hour	Summary of Events and Information	Remarks and references to Appendices
18		Batteries were occupied in preparing new positions W of HEBUTERNE	58.
19		One section of A, B, C & D Batteries relieved by a section of corresponding batteries of 162 Bde RFA & marched to wagon lines at PAS. Guns of 78th Bde left in action, guns of 162 Bde RFA taken over. 78th Bde H.Q. was relieved by the 162 Bde RFA in NORTHERN GROUP remaining section of 78th Bde with ammn to wagon lines at PAS	
20		78th Bde marched from wagon lines at PAS to FROHEN-LE-GRAND at 8.50 a.m. arriving at 1.30 p.m. were billeted in the village.	MAP LENS 11 1/100000
21		78th Brigade marched to training area at 1.15 p.m. & billeted as follows. H.Q. in AUXI-LE-CHATEAU A Battery in WILLENCOURT B Battery in LA NEUVILLE C Battery in WILLENCOURT D Battery in AUXI.	
22			
23		Brigade at rest in AUXI-LE-CHATEAU area.	

WAR DIARY
INTELLIGENCE SUMMARY

78th Bde. RFA

September 1916

Army Form C. 2118

Place	Date	Hour	Summary of Events and Information	Remarks and references to Appendices
	24		Brigade in rest at AUXI-LE-CHATEAU-ones.	
	25		" " " " " "	
	26		" " " " " "	
	27		" " " " " "	
	28		" " " " " " orders rcvd to be ready to move at an hours notice from 8 AM 29.9.16.	
	29		Brigade marched to OCCOCHES. + was billeted there for the night.	
	30		Brigade marched to PAS. HUTS. via DOULLENS. working parties sent forward to complete preparation of wire cutting positions near HEDAUTERNE.	

Ammunition Expended by Batteries during September 1916

A. Battery. 653 A   C Battery   22 YA.   Signed [illegible]
             YF6 Ax.   23 YAx.   Comdg. 78th Bde RFA
             326 A   95 BX
B   "   266 Ax.   D "   55 PBP

Army Form C. 2118

Vol 76

76. BDE. RFA. 60.

WAR DIARY
or
INTELLIGENCE SUMMARY
(Erase heading not required.)

OCTOBER 1916

Place	Date	Hour	Summary of Events and Information	Remarks and references to Appendices
HEBUTERNE	1.		Brigade at PAS. HUTS. Working parties engaged in making new battery positions near Jones the Bypass. LT. D.A. NICOLL and 2nd LT. W.F. PARRINGTON joined the Brigade.	Map 57D NE
	2.		Brigade at PAS. HUTS. Working parties working on new positions	
	3.		Brigade moved into the line, and took up the following positions. H.Qrs. K.7.C.5.5. "A". K.2.C.6.6. (2 guns) K.6.B.9.8. (4 guns) "B". K.6.4.6.6. (6 guns) "C". K.2.C.3.3. (4 guns) K.15.D.2.4. (2 guns) D. J.12.D.2.2. (4 guns)	
	4.		Brigade cutting from K.4.D.2.7 to K.1.A.3.6 for wire cutting on above zone. Practically no hostile retaliation. Brigade started wire cutting on defences of the line from K.5.D.70.70 to K.10.B.95.95.	
	5.		At 10 A.M. 76/Brigade took over defence of the line from K.5.D.70.70 to K.10.B.95.95. All guns registered on front line, and howitzer Battery on trench junctions in support line. Continued wire cutting. Very little hostile retaliation	

Army Form C. 2118

WAR DIARY
or
INTELLIGENCE SUMMARY
(Erase heading not required.)

OCTOBER 1916   T 8 Bar R.F.A.

Place	Date	Hour	Summary of Events and Information	Remarks and references to Appendices
HEBUTERNE	6		18 pdr. batteries occupied in wire cutting D/78 fired in retaliation for hostile trench mortaring.	Map 57D NE
"	7		18 pdr. batteries occupied in wire cutting during the morning D/78 fired in retaliation for hostile trench mortaring.	
"	8		Bees occupied in wire cutting 60 rds. per gun per diem.	
"	9		" " " 60 " " " "	
"	10		" " " 40 " " " "	
"	11		" " " 40 " " " "	
"	12		" " " 40 " " " "	
			Bae also occupied in keeping gaps open at night by intermittent shelling & renewing firelines.	

Army Form C. 2118

WAR DIARY
or
INTELLIGENCE SUMMARY

78th. Bde. R.F.A.

October 1916

(Erase heading not required.)

62

Place	Date	Hour	Summary of Events and Information	Remarks and references to Appendices
HEBUTERNE	13.		Wire cutting continued + night firing on gaps in wire.	
"	14		Wire cutting continued. Night firing on gaps	
"	15		" " " " "	
"	16		Wire cutting continued " " "	
PAS	17		The 78th. Bde withdrew from the line in front of GOMMECOURT at 7 p.m. marched to wagon lines at PAS bivouacing for the night.	Map LENS No. 11
ALBERT	18.		The 78th Bde marched to vicinity of ALBERT at 10 a.m. via FAMECHON SARTON MARIEUX - ARQUEVES - LEALVILLERS - VARENNES - SENLIS. Bde bivouaced at W29 a central. Bde + battery commanders made reconnaissance of Bde area.	
"	19		Battery positions being prepared on fronts A/R32 a 85 B/R31 b 15 R31 d 78 D/R32 C 42 5TDSE + Bde. H.Q at X2a 47	
"	20		Work continued on battery positions + batteries moved actions into new positions J.T.	

Army Form C. 2118

WAR DIARY
or
INTELLIGENCE SUMMARY
(Erase heading not required.)

78th Bde. R.F.A.   OCTOBER 1916.   63

Place	Date	Hour	Summary of Events and Information	Remarks and references to Appendices
	21		Batteries moved resuming actions into position + were occupied dumping ammunition up to 650 rds per 18 pr. & 70 per 4.5" HW.	Map 57D SE
	22		Dumping of ammunition continued	"
	23		Bde. H.Q. moved to H.Q. at X.29.4.7. and Bde. 150ft over the line from X.21.9.15 to X.21.6.1.5 in front of GRANDCOURT. and all guns registered. Wire cutting commenced by Bde. 3pm but very little wire can be seen.	"
	24		01.6 a.m. A + C batteries + 2 Hows of D/78 opened an intense barrage bombardment on roads leaving GRAND COURT firing 720 rds 18 pr + 60 rds 5X. Intermittent fire kept up during day on enemy works + on new trenches at night	"
	25		All Batteries engaged firing on new trenches roads, also BAILLESCOURT FARM and MIRAUMONT night firing carried out on enemy new trenches.	"
	26		Wire cutting continued about R15c78. Day and night firing carried out over zone.	"
	27		Wire cutting continued at R15C78 and from R15 a 73 — R15f57 — day night firing carried out on roads, communication trenches + new works	"
	28		Bde. Zone shelled intermittently day night + wire cutting continued.	"
	29			

WAR DIARY or INTELLIGENCE SUMMARY

Army Form C. 2118

78th Bde. R.F.A.

OCTOBER 1916

Place	Date	Hour	Summary of Events and Information	Remarks and references to Appendices
M/THIEPVAL	30		Day night firing carried out on enemy's work roads. During day A + C batteries occupied in wire cutting.	Map 57D.S.E. 64.
M/THIEPVAL	31.		Bde occupied in cutting wire in Bn zone during day & intermittingly shelling all roads + trenches to prevent enemy work + movement. Gun battles batteries engaged an aeroplane call at 4.10 p.m. barraged enemy's front line on heavy shelling of our trenches. Fire ceased at 4.35 p.m. During night all quiet.	"

J. George Holden
Lt Col.
Commdg 78th Bde R.F.A.

1/11/16

WAR DIARY or INTELLIGENCE SUMMARY

Army Form C. 2118.

Vol 17
78th Bde R.F.A.
65

November 1916

Place	Date	Hour	Summary of Events and Information	Remarks and references to Appendices
THIEPVAL	1.	12 mid/night	All batteries engaged in keeping roads, works & enemy trenches in Rgt at C & R 15 a, b, c & d under fire to prevent new work. Gaps cut in wire abandoned to prevent repair. A & C batteries engaged hostile batteries. During the day wire cutting carried out about R15 central. Ammunition expended 1329 A 695 A × 58 BX.	Map. 57 D SE
	2.		All batteries engaged in keeping roads & trenches under fire firing about 700 per gun per 24 hours. A Battery continued wire cutting about R15 central. Practically no wire left - to the eastwith in Beaugne.	"
	3.		After many tanks carried out as before during the afternoon enemy aeroplane very active. Several of our batteries were shelled. A/78 was shelled & had a small ammunition dump blown up about 2.00 a.m. 18 Nov. Two men killed & few wounded.	"
	4.			"
	5.		Heavy day & night tasks carried out by the Brigade, road, new trenches, enemy front line kept continuously under fire. Great difficulty experienced in maintaining communication owing to the hues lies fire & wet condition of ground trenches. Hostile trench mortars TOG A 47 9 AX 96 BX no fire. Continued Tasks of keeping enemy under fire. Barrage across the AVOCE at RgaA 97 60 + Rga 8076.	"

WAR DIARY or INTELLIGENCE SUMMARY

Army Form C. 2118.

November 1916   78th Bde. R.F.A.

Place	Date	Hour	Summary of Events and Information	Remarks and references to Appendices
THIEPVAL	6		Fired day & night on zone to prevent work. Enemy barrages at R9a 78 + 96 registered by A + C Batteries. Enemy aeroplane mostly O.K's obtained. Enemy shelled our trenches fairly heavily all day with 77mm + 105mm Howr especially between SCHWABEN + STUFF Redoubts. 2 18pdr of B Battery sent to I.O.M worn out badly scored.	Maps 57 D SE
"	7		Fire kept up day & night on enemy trenches, gaps in wire, new works + the two bridges across the ANCRE at R9a 78 + 96. Weather very wet rain for observation. Bursts + hurricane fire between the ruins. STUFF REDOUBT shelled consistently with 5.9's. Two guns of A + C Batteries sent to I.O.M with worn pieces.	
"	8		During day & night kept enemy man fire + especially roads & bridges in zone at night. Gaps in wire shewn intermittently to prevent all wire.	
"	9		As on 8th. Also fired on 52cA 79.5Ax 152.BX	
"	10		As on 9th. Also fired 62qA 35.0Ax 100.Bx from 5.30 to 6.a.m bombarded GRANDCOURT + outskirts of village & communication Trenches leading thereto.	
"	11		From 5.30 a.m. to 6 a.m. bombarded enemy communication Trenches leading to GRANDCOURT. Enemy retaliated fairly heavily. During the day carried out continuous bombardment were cutting on wire front.	

2449 Wt. W14957/M90 750,000 1/16 J.B.C. & A. Forms/C.2118/12.

Army Form C. 2118.

WAR DIARY
or
INTELLIGENCE SUMMARY

(Erase heading not required.)

T/8th Bn R.F.A.

November 1916

Place	Date	Hour	Summary of Events and Information	Remarks and references to Appendices
THIEPVAL	12		From 5.30 – 6 a.m. bombarded enemy front line support with half the guns of the Bde. Enemy retaliated slightly. During the day bombarded intermittently all batteries, wire cutting, destruction of dug-outs, enemy wire. 18 pdr. 400 m per battery – 4.5" Hows 300 m per Bty. rate of fire 2 rds per 18 pdr per min – 1 rd per How per min.	Map 57d S.E. 67
	13		At 5.45 a.m. the Bde put up a creeping barrage as far as DESIRE Trench. Enemy operation on the N bank of the ANCRE. Wire & destruct the enemy retaliation. D/T.B. shelled STUMP ROAD u R15a + enclosures from R9c5.3 to R9d10. 7/S/R H.S. MARSH. Relieved.	
	14		A quiet day. Enemy made their repl man fire day rough	
	15		During day + night enemy works kept under fire to prevent all work. D/T.B. engages hostile battery in R4+909.	
	16		Enemy lines + communication + new works kept under fire.	

WAR DIARY or INTELLIGENCE SUMMARY

Army Form C. 2118.

78th Bde RFA

November 1916

Date	Hour	Summary of Events and Information	Remarks and references to Appendices
17		Group works + communications kept under fire right away.	Map 57 D.S.E 68
18		The attempted attack of 57th (part) and 55th (part) Inf. Bdes. at 6.10 a.m. by means of a rolling barrage across STUMP ROAD. D Battery shelled roads + communication trenches leading out of GRANDCOURT. At 6.30 a.m. a protective barrage was maintained to 10 a.m. from STUMP ROAD to 400 yds. due East. 2/Lt. H.F. DENHAM SMITH + 2 signallers missing of B/78 moving observation duty as liaison with 8th N. Staff'd R. A quiet day	
19			
20		At 7 a.m. the Brigade with drew from the line marched to wagon lines on BOUZINCOURT ALBERT road at W.20 central	
21		Bde marched at 9.30 a.m. to camp S.W. of MEAULTE	

Army Form C. 2118.

WAR DIARY
or
INTELLIGENCE SUMMARY
(Erase heading not required.)

Place: November 1916 — 18th Bde R.F.A.

Date	Hour	Summary of Events and Information	Remarks and references to Appendices
22		Bde in rest in camp S.W. of MEAULTE	MAP. CONBAYED SHEET ALBERT 1/40,000
23		Bde in rest in camp S.W. of MEAULTE	
24		Bde Commander reconnoitred position to be taken over from 33rd Bde. R.F.A.	
		Battery Commanders reconnoitred position to be taken over from 33 Bde R.F.A.	
25		Bde in rest near Méaulte.	
26		Bde marched to new wagon lines at 10.15 a.m. via FRICOURT & CARNOY to F.12.C. centre & there bivouacked for the night. During the morning 3 section of A.B.C. & 2 section of D battery relieved corresponding sections of 32nd, 33rd, 3rd & 55th Batteries of 33 Bde R.F.A.	Map 57C S.W.
27		Remaining sections of all batteries relieved remaining sections of batteries of 33rd Bde. All guns taken over stripped with exception of Dial sights, telescopes, sights & eight clinometers. Bde H.Q. relieved 33rd Bde H.Q. at 12 noon. Took over defence of the line from T.6.a.07 to N.35.d.33. Position occupied as follows: HQ T.2.00.54; A/78 Tqd32; B/78 Tqd21; C/78 Tqc.77 to Tqt.76; D/78 Tqd21.	"

Army Form C. 2118.

WAR DIARY
or
INTELLIGENCE SUMMARY
(Erase heading not required.)

Place: T&M Ray, RFA

Date	Hour	Summary of Events and Information	Remarks and references to Appendices
November 1916			
28		Very foggy. Area maintained on enemy's defences & by night all known roads kept under intermittent fire. Batteries occupied in improving position & communications.	Map 57cSW
29		All batteries shelled intermittently enemy defences SE of Pollux & SLEET trench.	"
30		During the night fire maintained on all roads & tracks in zone in view of probable enemy relief taking place. 200 rounds per 18 pdr battery & T.S.M. were then batteries fired. Ammunition fired during month 13351 A 10h25 AX 4110 BX Casualties:— 2/Lt. H.S. Marsh killed 15/11/16 2/Lt F.H. Denham Smith missing 15/11/16 O.Rs 3 killed O.Rs Wounded 15. O.Rs Missing 2. O.Rs Wounded at duty 2.	"

J.E. Grey, Lt Col
Cmdg 78th Bde RFA

WAR DIARY
or
INTELLIGENCE SUMMARY

Army Form C. 2118.

Vol 18

18th Bty. R.F.A. T1

December 1916

Place	Date	Hour	Summary of Events and Information	Remarks and references to Appendices
GIVENCHY	1.		Batteries engaged in improving position for A + D batteries about 200 yds in rear.	Map 57C S.W. T1
	2.		Batteries engaged in day & night firing on enemy front line support trenches in zone. All hostile work kept under fire during darkness.	"
	3.		ditto.	"
	4.		ditto.	"
	5.		During the day visibility very bad. During the night Divisional salvoes were fired on the following points N30c.14; O.19c.54; O.25c.64; O.31c.12.	"
	6.		Reconnaissance for O.P's from which enemy front line could be seen was carried out by all Battery Commanders. During night salvoes were fired on following points O.25c.5.3½; N.30b.8.2.6; O.25.a.1.2.0	"

WAR DIARY or INTELLIGENCE SUMMARY

Army Form C. 2118.

78th Bde RFA

December 1916

Place	Date	Hour	Summary of Events and Information	Remarks and references to Appendices
GINCHY	7		Enemy's trenches N36C. Reported own fire by 18pdrs. MOON trench bombarded by 7/78	Map FRANCE 57cSW
"	8		Bombarded trench areas in O31a & O xc & BAPAUME road about O36a88	"
"	9		One 4.5 How of D/78 destroyed by direct hit of 4.2 How which detonated 60 rounds of Bx in emplacement. No casualties	"
"	10		78th Bde RFA maintains enemy's front line support trenches kept under intermittent burst of fire D/78 bombarded MOON TRENCH.	"
MEAULTE	11		79th Bde relieved the 78th Bde RFA in the line. 78th Bde marched to Camp on MEAULTE – MORLANCOURT road at F28C vacated by the 79th Bde RFA.	ALBERT Continued sheet
MORLAN-COURT	12		78th Bde RFA moved to rest billets in MORLANCOURT.	1/40000
"	13		Bde. in rest	"
"	14		Bde. in rest	"
"	15		Bde. in rest	"

WAR DIARY
or
INTELLIGENCE SUMMARY

Army Form C. 2118.

18th Bde. RFA

Place	Date	Hour	Summary of Events and Information	Remarks and references to Appendices
MORLANCOURT	16th		Bde in rest	AUBERT Contoured Sheet 1/40,000
"	17th		"	"
"	18th		"	"
"	19th		"	"
"	20th		"	"
"	21st		"	"
"	22nd		"	"
"	23rd		"	"
"	24th		"	"
"	25th		"	"
"	26th		Advance party consisting of all Officers & signallers per battery & Headquarters went down to SLOTTS 18 RFA in preparation for taking over	"

Army Form C. 2118.

WAR DIARY
or
INTELLIGENCE SUMMARY

(Erase heading not required.)

December 1916   78th Bde R.F.A.

Place	Date	Hour	Summary of Events and Information	Remarks and references to Appendices
GINCHY	27th		Half batteries 78th Bde marched to 2nd wagon lines CARNOY E20 c/78. CARNOY E20 c/78 which remained in rear at MORLANCOURT.	Map France 57C SW
	28th		Half batteries relieved half batteries of 81st Bde in the line, guns being drawn in. Running half batteries E20 c/78 marched from MORLANCOURT to CARNOY.	"
	29th		Running half batteries + Headquarters relieved remaining half batteries of 81st + Headquarters at 12 noon.	"
	30th		Batteries engaged in keeping enemy wire cutting fire in the zone N 36 b 55 – O 21 c 20 – O 28 O 27 d 96 – U 19 a 36.	"
	31st		Bombarded the area U19 18 80 – U1 a 00 85 – O3 c 95 80 – O3 d 9 36 from 2 p.m to 2.30 p.m firing 45A + 135 AX per 18 pr battery + 120 BX per H.M. Battery. During the night bombarded with bursts of fire every 15 minutes the ground in O 31 a wording the way O 2 s d. At 12 noon fired retaliation S.O.S fire on cruiser O 3 O O O O O.	
			Ammunition Expended during Month :- 2015A 3363AX 232 CBX	
			Casualties :- 1 O.R. wounded.	

Alfred Gay Capt.
Lt. Col.
Cmmdg 78th Bde R.F.A.

January 1st 1917

WAR DIARY or INTELLIGENCE SUMMARY

Army Form C. 2118.

78th Bde RFA

Place	Date	Hour	Summary of Events and Information	Remarks and references to Appendices
GINCHY	1.		Day firing 100 AX and 50 A into LE TRANSLOY and 150 BX into O.31.b. Night-firing 80 A + 75 AX on trenches at O.25.c. 16.25.t + BAPAUME Rd.	
	2.		Day firing 50 A and 100 AX into O.31.c - 150 BX into O.31.b. Retaliation on LE TRANSLOY CEMETRY 11.45 AM and on Sunken road N.36.a at 1.5 p.m. Hostile fire normal - MORVAL + LES BŒUFS shelled intermittently during the day. Night-firing 80 A 250 AX fired on trenches in O.31.b in short bursts. Hostile fire normal -	

WAR DIARY or INTELLIGENCE SUMMARY

Army Form C. 2118.

18th Bde R.F.A

JANUARY 1917

Place	Date	Hour	Summary of Events and Information	Remarks and references to Appendices
GINCHY	3.		Day firing 80 A + 150 AX on trenches at O25c - 150 BX on windmill in O31c fired in short bursts. During the night - Tracks between ROCQUIGNY and BAPAUME R⁴ kept under intermittent bursts of fire.	
"	4.		Day firing – 18 Pdrs + 2 bursts of fire on WINDMILL & trenches in O31a & 4.5 Hows shelled dump & road in O25c. Answer "6" fired in retaliation. Night - firing 50A and 150 AX on U25-08 to O33c06 - 4.5 How 150 BX on SUNKEN RD in O33a + 6 –	
"	5.		Day firing 50A + 150 AX fired in bursts on SUNKEN R⁴ and tracks in O33 4.C.7 Bombardment - as per O.O. N⁰ 9 carried out from 1.20 p.m. to 1.55 p.m. – A/78 front line trench from T.6a05.90 to T.6b85.95 – B/78 from T5b85.95 to N35d70.00 – D/78 Strong point T6a0593 Night - firing 18 Pdrs on trenches U25.08 & O33c06 – 4.5 How on Sunken Rd in O33a4.	
"	6		Day firing 18 Pdrs on back areas & strafing allotment 200 AX – 4.5 Hows 50 BX on outskirts of ROCQUIGNY and opportunity targets	
"	7		C.O. N⁰ 11 carried out 12.6 12.48 p.m. D/78 fired on trench N3b 85.00 to U1a 03. 97. During ⚒ must also were seen a engaged by 18 pdrs targets into a back areas. Night firing 200 AX all trenches Day firing was carried out U0321 + U2 + 100 BX into ROCQUIGNY & outskirts.	
"	8.		At 8 am B/79 & 97⁴ Bty joined the Right Group on its taking over the defence of the zone U2.C.4.1. – U.11. a 4.9 aeroplane went over the Day firing under roads & track areas shelled with AX & ROCQUIGNY with 700 BX Night firing 100 A & 500 AX on trenches tracks in O32933 4U293 150 BX into ROCQUIGNY outskirts	

Army Form C. 2118.

WAR DIARY
or
INTELLIGENCE SUMMARY

(Erase heading not required.)

78th Bde R.F.A.

January 1917

Place	Date	Hour	Summary of Events and Information	Remarks and references to Appendices
GINCHY	9		O.O. No 13 carried out. D/78 bombarded MOON Trench N.36.d.; B/79 & 97² swept ground in rear of trench. Day firing 100A & 200AX into trenches & tracks & then cheo in 031.402 & 50 BX. N.G. ROCQUIG -NY. Night firing 200A & 300 AX onto tracks & then cheo in 032.933, 402.43. & 4 MOON Trench & in addition shot bombardments of 3 rounds gunfire – 031.402 all guns in the group on roads in 026 & B27 & woods in 031.402 from 4:30 to 7:0 a.m. A/78 & Howitzery T.16.a was lightly shelled with 10.5 cm. gas shell (phosgene). No damage to personnel or material.	
	10		Day firing trenches on 031.932 & LE TRANSLOY-ROCQUIGNY road. Night firing trenches dugouts & tracks in 026.31.932 & ROCQUIGNY & also short bombardments on ROCQUIGNY trenches in 031.927	
	11		Daytime enemy reply stronger in 026.31.932 shelled ROCQUIGNY-LE TRANSLOY Road with intensity & BX. Night firing trenches tracks & roads in 031,32 & U.2 shelled with 16 phos. & ROCP 01.3 BX, & LE TRANSLOY with howitzers.	
	12		Day firing – harass & fire on unknown roads trenches in Bde zone. O.O. No 15. Night firing trenches dugouts country tracks at 2.0 pm hostile retaliation. Night firing trenches & areas subjected to desultory delayed fire. ROCQUIGNY, LE TRANSLOY Roads shelled with BX.	
	13		Daytime trenches in Bde zone shelled intro ROCQUIGNY. O.O. No 14 fired at 12.48 pm. Retaliation not very much. Night firing harassing fire kept up on tracks & track areas. Intermittent fire on roads & trenches in Bde zone.	
	14		Day firing as usual on trenches trenches junction roads in Bde zone. During night burst of fire on back areas & well RJ PROMETHEUS, FURIES and SCHUMANN Trenches. Thirty see Jay & B/79 reported their new zone.	

WAR DIARY
or
INTELLIGENCE SUMMARY

Army Form C. 2118.

Place	Date	Hour	Summary of Events and Information	Remarks and references to Appendices
GINCHY	15.1.17		Visibility fair. "L" Bty reported usual intermittent shelling by 19 Pdrs others nil. Day. 5 rounds in DECAUVILLE Railway 10.5.5. Night firing as usual on track areas Windmill normal & approaches to ROCQUIGNY. Enemy artillery activity below normal.	
"	16.1.17		Visibility poor. C Bty test their SOS lines. Day firing as usual. Night firing Group Salvos ordered by 17 Divr. if any enemy relief is expected. LBty 5 O.R. wounded by 15cm. Usual night firing in back areas. Enemy artillery activity normal.	
"	17/1/17		Enemy tracks and Roads under intermittent fire day & night	
"	18/1/17		Visibility very poor. During 14° night - trenches in U.16 & O.31 shelled by 18Pdr & 4.5 How also trenches in their vicinity - ROCQUIGNY also shelled by 4.5s. Hostile fire below normal. BOULEAUX wood shelled at times by a hostile 15cm gun.	
"	19/1/17		Visibility fairly good. Weather bad in the afternoon. C Bty acted when S.O.S. barrage & HBty calibrated & registered various Roads. During night fire directed on U.26, U.32.C. & during the day 18 Pdrs & 4.5 Hows. intermittently shelled the outskirts of ROCQUIGNY. Hostile fire above normal, T.13. C.30 & T.19.a.o.b shelled with 7.7 cm gun. during the morning. Some rounds of 8 cm. 077 Ccm. fell around Festin.	

D/78.

WAR DIARY or INTELLIGENCE SUMMARY

Army Form C. 2118.

Place	Date	Hour	Summary of Events and Information	Remarks and references to Appendices
QUOENY	20/11/17		Practice barrage carried out at 3.15 P.M. this afternoon by B/78, B/78 split up into groups re-organized & brought carried of of 2 Bde SHERBROKE commanding 15th Bde. A/78 - A/78 + B/78 Battery the Group organized & replaced by "B" "D.9" and WARWICK 18th R.H.A. respectively - 78th Bde A.9. Temporarily disbanded —	
"	21/11/17		Visibility fair. Usual day & night firing carried out on enemy tracks & trenches.	
"	22/11/17		D/78 Brigade a 6gun battery obtaining 2 guns from D/21-78th H.Q. still temporarily dismounted & group unable to be of service for tactical purposes. All firing beyond registration. Fineling operation. Batteries worked on getting ammunition up to establishment.	
"	23/11/17		H.Q. Staff split up & not being used as a 78th H.Q.	
"	24/11/17		Practice barrage & S.O.S. lines at 3.15 P.M. attack of unknown successfully carried out & hour's gun fire.	
"	25/11/17		Visibility fair. Registration leaving & battery calibrated as much as possible. Operation against hostile trenches at U.36.C piece successfully carried out with small losses on own side — attack was launched at 5.30 a.m. under a screen of Shrapnel — H.E. and a very successful screen of M.G. smoke shell behind which B/78 cooperation from consolidated & two new hostile counter attacks Mud making every new position infantry obtained bowing up & consolidating new front line trenches	

| " | 26/11/17 | | | |

WAR DIARY
or
INTELLIGENCE SUMMARY

(Erase heading not required.)

Army Form C. 2118.

Instructions regarding War Diaries and Intelligence Summaries are contained in F. S. Regs., Part II. and the Staff Manual respectively. Title Pages will be prepared in manuscript.

Place	Date	Hour	Summary of Events and Information	Remarks and references to Appendices
Guidy	29/1/17		During night enemy bombarded our new front line trenches. Our artillery retaliated after a short time all firing died down. During day hostile fire fairly incessant. Our ammunition dump blown up in position 6)'L' 15.89. Our fire was in receipt of order to economise ammunition. Hostile fire below normal, a few rounds fired put into MORVAL. 7.00) spot visibility poor.	
"	30/1/17		Work was carried on all day in improving gun positions.	
"	31/1/17		During night, a few bursts of fire from Bples of troops in Jones's back area. A Hpa? T3/T8 carried out calibration satisfactorily. Hostile aircraft very active.	
"	1/2/17		Usual night firing carried out. Hostile fire below normal. Enemy aircraft active, & one of his planes was sent to its come down behind his lines, apparently hit by A.A shell. Visibility fair.	
"	2/2/17		Calibration & registration carried out on Rosnia trench.	

WAR DIARY or INTELLIGENCE SUMMARY

Army Form C. 2118.

78th BRIGADE R.F.A. Vol 20

Place	Date	Hour	Summary of Events and Information	Remarks and references to Appendices
Ginchy	1/2/17		Usual night firing carried out. Hostile fire below normal. Enemy aircraft active. One of his planes was seen to fall behind his lines approx. Shot 57°S.W. hit by our A.A. guns. Visibility fair. J.G.R.	Trench Map Shot 57°S.W. 1/20,000
"	2/2/17		Calibration & registration carried out on BOSNIA TRENCH & S.O.S. lines checked. Hostile fire above normal. Heavy burst on B Head Bari-night M/G & TRANSLOY wheel exact for about 15 minutes. Visibility poor. J.G.R.	
"	3/2/17		Few enemy aircraft active over front line & batteries. Our artillery activity low. all guns calibrated for line & range. Barrage fired for E.R.A. REDOUBT, and & WAKES fired on by our 4.5 How. Hostile fire considerably below normal. Occasional rounds in MORVAL & LESBŒUFS. Visibility low. Enemy aircraft active 18 pdrs until their S.O.S. barrage. J.G.R.	
"	4/2/17		ROCQUIGNY. Hostile fire above normal - 4.5 How fired on trenches & approaches to ROCQUIGNY. Hostile fire above normal - 7 pdr somewhat heavily shelled at by 6pdr + 4.1 HV guns. She had direct hit on signallers dug-out & gunner being killed and one wounded. Hostile aircraft very active. During the morning we observed to hit a rifle position from our Anti-Aircraft gun between MORVAL & LESBŒUFS. S.O.S barrages practised at U, & U2. During the night Bungalow on trenches in 0.31.3.2 and trenches in U, & U2 - Hostile fire behind MORVAL 7.5d was shelled at intervals by 67gm. Hostile aeroplane active one flying very low at about 50m over MORVAL & LESBŒUFS. Visibility poor. J.G.R.	
"	5.2.17			

Army Form C. 2118.

Instructions regarding War Diaries and Intelligence Summaries are contained in F. S. Regs., Part II. and the Staff Manual respectively. Title Pages will be prepared in manuscript.

WAR DIARY
or
INTELLIGENCE SUMMARY
(Erase heading not required.)

Place	Date	Hour	Summary of Events and Information	Remarks and references to Appendices
GINCHY	6-2-17		Night firing as usual – 108 rounds fired on trenches in H1 & b. During the day S.O.S. lines tested by F.O.Bs in front line. The batteries fired on two targets on cattle from the air. Hostile fire below normal. 8/78 moved into forward position near the ORCHARD at MORVAL. During the night – two guns to forward position near the ORCHARD at MORVAL. During the night. Visibility poor.	SGK
"	7/2/17		During the night – bursts of fire by 18 Pdrs on tracks and back areas in our gone F.A.5. Hours shelled approaches to ROCQUIGNY. During the day batteries registered. BOSNIA salient in U.b.r.d. Hostile fire above normal. 8/78 shelled intermittently by S.1 & 9.1 H.V. guns. A/93 & 97th Batteries gained the Group positions between 11am & 12 noon. Hostile planes active over battery positions between 11am & 12 noon during the evening. Night firing as normal. At 7:30 a.m. barrages carried out in accordance with A.O.21 with 5hr shrapnel by 18 Pdrs & Smoke shell by 4.5 Hows. The enemy put up a feeble retaliation to own barrages — but from 10 a.m. onwards throughout the day SAILLY-SAILLISEL bombarded regularly with guns of all calibre. At 10 am two ALBATROSS & two S.E.Ss. patrolling MORVAL. They were unmolested & still patrolling MORVAL at 11.30 a.m. At 3.15 three planes were	SGK
"	8-2-17		observed by B^E aeroplane scout – flying very low over our lines. They were dispersed by our anti-aircraft guns. Retaliation carried out on S.O.S. lines during the night. During day activities also carried out registration. Hostile fire normal. 9.1s & 4.1s shelled by S.9 H.V. guns. Visibility	SGK
"	9-2-17			

WAR DIARY or INTELLIGENCE SUMMARY

Army Form C. 2118.

Place	Date	Hour	Summary of Events and Information	Remarks and references to Appendices
SINIETY	10th		Bombardment carried out by all batteries on posn: S.O.2.D on BOSNIA Salient. W.b.t.d. + reported by F.O.O's as very effective. In retaliation to our fire the enemy shelled CROWN SUPPORT in aid from 2.15 p.m. to 3.30 p.m. His barrage was thin + not very concentrated at any time + from 10 a.m. to 12 noon two S.P.H.V. guns firing a very small dropped several shells about T76 & T. Hostile aeroplanes very active during the bombardment. One plane flew over battery pos[itio]n + was noted to have a black broad white and blue stripe, another was noted to have a black broad with a shiny character. At 5.30 p.m. retaliation carried out by all batteries in response to call from infantry. During the night fire was directed on tracks + buildings in Y.2 & T.16. The 18 pdrs fired 75 rounds + the 4.5 how. 125 rounds. In retaliation 098 carried out two Test Charges from Inglesby. The enemy seemed very nervous + replied to bombardment on BOSNIA in W.b.t.d. Hostile fire however normal. 18 an hour registered T76.35 by plane.	SGK
"	11th		at 7.10 a.m. & 10.45 a.m. – Visibility low.	SGK
"	12th		During the night 6/78 received on Dot Call at 10.7 which was answered in under one minute. 29/78 fired 60BX to PROMETHEUS Trench and roads and tracks in our front. Hostile fire much below normal – practically no hostile fire on our front during the past 24 hrs. Visibility low.	SGK
"	13th		BOSNIA Trench reported by all Batteries on shoot firing with T/6a below normal. T/6a shelled from 10–10.30 am by 77m guns on T/6a. S.1. Smoke bearing 170°, latter 5.93.4.42.5 and burst of fire by 77m guns from T.156 43.00 or 64°.1 Visibility poor.	SGK

2449 Wt. W14957/M90 750,000 1/16 J.B.C. & A. Forms/C.2118/12.

WAR DIARY or INTELLIGENCE SUMMARY

Army Form C. 2118.

Place	Date	Hour	Summary of Events and Information	Remarks and references to Appendices
GINCHY	14th		During the night 4.5 How. fired 60 BX on Trench mortars reported by Liason Officer which were effectively silenced. 18 Pdrs. fired a Destruct. Call from the Infantry - time taken 33 sec. At 10.30 a.m. 7.0.0 reported heavy hostile rifle grenade fire from BOSNIA, 6/78 forward guns fired 25 rounds into this trench which effectively stopped the enemy firing. Rate of fire below normal. 75 rounds 7.7cm shells near Demonville Rly. at Y16.C. Volley on 7.St shelled at intervals. S.O.K	
	15th		Enemy Aircraft very active and flying much lower than usual. Visibility fair. 18 Pdrs fired intermittently on Sniping Post in V.2.c.1.7.; enemy dump at V.2.b.2.3 and near of BOSNIA during the night and 4.5" How. fired 120 BX in 6 salvos at T.M.'s reported by the Infantry at V.1.6.6.5. S.O.S. line checked 7 guns calibrated during the day. Working Party fired on by 6/78 at O.31.c.4.2. Hostile fire rather above normal. Our front line shelled by 4.2s + 5.9s. Right Btn. H.Q. shelled during the morning. About 7.30 p.m. last evening enemy planes flying high dropped three golden lights over 6/78 forward position. Hostile flares + balloons very active. 36 planes being observed during the day. Visibility fair to good. S.O.K.	
	16th		Last night about 6.30 p.m. two T.M.'s were reported very active at V.1.a.8.8 + O.31.c.2.5. D/75 with 4.5 How. of the Left Group fired 4 salvos. B/12 How. at East Point Major bright D/75 with 4.5 burst the front line trenches during the night and he was informed by the Inf. Coy Comdrs. that this firing was very accurate and also that no further firing by T.M.'s had taken place. 18 Pdrs. fired on Working Party at O.31.c.4.2 during the morning. 6/78 dispersed at Working Party at O.31.c.4.2. Hostile fire above normal. At 7.30 p.m. Bttn. H.Q. at T.17.d.73 was shelled by 4.2. 20 guns from direction of ST. PIERRE VAAST WOOD. On front line shelled intermittently and	

WAR DIARY
or
INTELLIGENCE SUMMARY

Army Form C. 2118.

Place	Date	Hour	Summary of Events and Information	Remarks and references to Appendices
GINCHY	16th Contd.		and 5.9: several rounds around GINCHY and also in T.16. Visibility variable. Hostile aircraft very active until 3 p.m. when they were driven away by our planes. 12 Hostile balloons observed. Our A/A appeared to be using a new type of gun of larger calibre and higher m.v. Sopwith planes were observed for the first time on this front.	
"	17th		Last night our H.S. Bns were with 8 hrs of left Group again fired active on T.M.'s reported active at U18.7.5. The enemy reported effective. Hrs also fired on SCHUMANN & PROMETHEUS Trenches throughout the night. 6/78 received 3 Dir Cartos from the Infantry - time taken 15 secs. 38 secs & 27 secs. Hostile fire below normal. About 3 am T16c was fired on for half an hour by 15 cm.	
"	18th		10 rounds & 7.7 cm - 50 rounds apparently in retaliation for 4.5 Hrs fire. 4.5 Hrs fired on T.M.s & on roads tracks from RUCQUIGNY. Hostile fire practically nil. Observation impossible owing to thick mist.	
"	19th		6/78 both parts in a bombardment on LE MESNIL 4.5 Hrs fired 50 Bx on SAXON & ANHALT trenches. Hostile fire much below normal. T11d was all day by 4.2 cm Hrs about 2 rounds every 5 minutes. Observation impossible owing to a thick mist nearly all the day.	

WAR DIARY
or
INTELLIGENCE SUMMARY.
(Erase heading not required.)

Army Form C. 2118.

Place	Date	Hour	Summary of Events and Information	Remarks and references to Appendices
GINCHY.	20.		All Batteries fired on "S.O.S NEW" on order from D. Arty. from 7.25 p.m. to a slow rate till 9 p.m. last evening. T.M's were fired on by D/78 at 2.30 a.m, 3.30, & 7.20 am. 6/78 fired bursts on ROCQUIGNY during the night. Hostile fire above normal. I Star continuous barrage from 4 am 19/2/17 till 2am 20/2/17 was carried out North-East of T.17 & 8.8. T.16 c & T.12 a + b were shelled intermittently by 15cm & 10.5 cm Valley about T.23 b was fired on from 10pm till midnight with 15cm Gas shrapnel shells. Visibility bad - a thick mist seen all day. SYK	
	21.		Day firing by Hows. on BOSNIA - 100 Bx. + Sabots during the night on T.M emplacements. All batteries fired on SCHUMANN, FURIES & PROMETHEUS trenches through the night. Hostile fire been normal. Visibility bad. SYK	
	22.		Retaliation for Enemy's barrage carried out by all batteries at 6 p.m. During the night A/78 fired on GALLIA trench & HAMMER COPSE. B/78 on FURIES & PROMETHEUS trenches. C/78 on ROCQUIGNY & MESNIL tracks leading to these places. D/78 on STAR TRENCH & T.M.S.	

WAR DIARY or INTELLIGENCE SUMMARY

Army Form C. 2118.

Place	Date	Hour	Summary of Events and Information	Remarks and references to Appendices
GINCHY	22 contd.		Hostile fire below normal. About 6 pm Enemy put up a medium barrage from SAILLY along the front line trenches of the Right Bttn. A great number of red lights were sent up throughout the bombardment by the enemy infantry along the whole area of the shelling. The bombardment began upon Silver rain rockets being sent up by their infantry. Unluckily there must prevailed all day. The 6/0 Left Bttn received reports from his Coy. Comdrs that the shooting of B/78 had been very effective. SOK	
	23		All Batteries fired "Retaliation" for 5 minutes at 2.30 pm at the request of the Infantry as the enemy was on our front line at CORD ALLEY. At 8.40 pm (23) all Btys fired 5 rounds gun fire on SOS lines in Retaliation for fire on Right Bttn trenches. The Infantry asked for further retaliation at 9.10 pm - A/78 & B/78 fired on their SOS lines. C/78 on ROCQUIGNY & D/78 on PROMETHEUS TRENCH - 2 minutes gun fire. Hostile fire about normal. In addition to the bombardment of our front line T.16.t - ORCHARD & DECEAUVILLE RLY were shelled	

Army Form C. 2118.

WAR DIARY
or
INTELLIGENCE SUMMARY.
(Erase heading not required.)

Instructions regarding War Diaries and Intelligence Summaries are contained in F. S. Regs., Part II. and the Staff Manual respectively. Title pages will be prepared in manuscript.

Place	Date	Hour	Summary of Events and Information	Remarks and references to Appendices
GINCHY	23	Cont'd	intermittently. Visibility very bad.	SLK
"	24		Night firing was carried out on roads leading to ROCQUIGNY + MESNIL HAMMER COPSE, dug-outs at U.26.2.5. 2/78 fired salvos & T.Ms in U.I.F. During the day 90 was carried out by A + D Btys. A fired 50A + 50AK on Trenches to N.36d & O.31c. D fired medium rate from 3.15pm - 4.15pm. C/78 carried out wire cutting at BOSNIA during the morning but low visibility rendered observation very difficult and impossible after 1 pm. Hostile fire below normal. In reply to an bombardment Ts 6 + T6a were shelled by 15cm + 10.5cm Btys, but their reply was by no means heavy. Pressure of gas shells were fired at various points during the night. Visibility low.	SLK
"	25		Night firing carried out by all Btys on roads leading in our zone. H/78 also fired on dugouts U.26.0.5. + U.3a.5.2. + 2/78 on SAXON TRENCH. RAXX carried out stable fire below normal. Visibility poor except at short intervals. U/317 C/78 cut wire on South side of BOSNIA during time observation was possible	SLK

T2134. W1. W708-776. 500 000. 4/15. Sir J. C. & S.

WAR DIARY or INTELLIGENCE SUMMARY

Army Form C. 2118.

Place	Date	Hour	Summary of Events and Information	Remarks and references to Appendices
GINCHY	26th		Night firing on truck and strikes on our gun and on the Southern exits from ROCQUIGNY & LE TRANSLOY. C/78 completed tasks of wirecutting at BOSNIA. 2/Lt. A.M.WOODS & 6696 Bdr. J.W.GASKIN were killed while carrying forward observation for this task. Hostile fire above normal. At 5.30 pm (26th) Enemy opened a heavy barrage on SAILLY-SAILLISEL lasting about 10 minutes. T.17.A was shelled by 77 mm gun shells (PHOS(GENE)). Hostile aircraft fairly active – 3 machines at 2.35 pm & 3 at 3.45 pm patrolled our front line & Bty. positions without being interrupted. S.t.B.K	
"	27th		During the night Btys. fired as follows A/78 on tracks refugepits, B/78 on BOSNIA TRENCH & ROCQUIGNY & MESNIL; B/78 on STAR & FURIES TRENCHES D/78 on tracks tracks. Enemy reported Enemy relief A, B/ + D/ fired on SOS lines & "Counter Preparation S". During the day C/76 Cut wire at N.36.d. – 137 rounds were expended. Hostile fire above normal. Left Bttn. HQ periodically shelled & front line trenches. During the night 20 – 77mm – T.14 & 20 rounds. Back area were also swept by 10.5 cm guns. LEATHAL shells in T.15 & T.14 & 20 rounds. Visibility good. Hostile aircraft active – 4 hlane flew low over	

Army Form C. 2118.

WAR DIARY
or
INTELLIGENCE SUMMARY.
(Erase heading not required.)

Place	Date	Hour	Summary of Events and Information	Remarks and references to Appendices
GINCHY	27th Contd		OP's + Bty. positions - they were not engaged by A/A guns, and they were having machine gun fire.	
	28th		During the night normal firing by all Btys. At 5.25 am O/O 26 & 27 were carried out as follows - A/78. B/78. C/78 places a barrage & enemys front line from U.8.6.30.40 - U.a.87.05 enemy front 80 rounds in the hour. D/78 on sector on BOSNIA SALIENT, 2 sections put up Smoke barrage from N.36.d.50.25 - N.36.b.50.10 to prevent enemy observation East of the line. The Barrage from V.8 - V.2 was reported exceedingly good. Hostile fire rather above normal. There reply to our firing this morning was fairly heavy and SAILLY-SAILLISEL but not very heavy on the left (N.36). During the morning the valley in T.15.b was shelled intermittingly by 4.2 guns. Occasional rounds in T.16.d. Visibility low - ground mist prevented observation.	

Ammunition Expenditure for month of January —

A Bx BSS Casualties
A.K. A.K. 350 Officer 1 (Killed)
4898 8653 5139   OR's 4 " 4 wounded.

J.W.M. Witts Lt Col RFA

WAR DIARY or INTELLIGENCE SUMMARY

78th BRIGADE R.F.A.

MARCH 1917

Army Form C. 2118.

Vol 2

Place	Date	Hour	Summary of Events and Information	Remarks and references to Appendices
GINCHY	MARCH 1		During the night normal night firing carried out by all Btys. on roads & tracks in our Brigade Zone – ROCQUIGNY & LE MESNIL also fired on wire bursts throughout the night. Rifle fire below normal – occasional S.O.S shells in vicinity of Bty. positions.	WD
	2		Normal night firing carried out. The first half Battery were relieved by opposite number of the Brigade – the 78th Bgde firing out half the number of guns of the 9th Brigade. Both fire below normal. Visibility poor.	WD
	3		The remaining Guns of the 9th Bde were brought out and the relief completed. The Brigade remained at the bivouac line at CARNOY as the order to proceeding to Rest Area was cancelled.	WD
CARNOY	4		The Brigade remained at CARNOY. Battery Commdrs. of D/78 + D/78 met the Brigade Commdr. at MARTINPUICH. Battery Commdrs. of B/78 + D/78 met the Brigade Commdr. at MARTINPUICH and new positions were selected.	WD
"+ ALBERT"	5		Brigade left W.L's at CARNOY at 7 a.m. to march to new W.L's at ALBERT, all Btys arrived there by 11.45 a.m. under orders of the 2nd Corps on this day.	WD

Army Form C. 2118.

WAR DIARY
or
INTELLIGENCE SUMMARY.
(Erase heading not required.)

Instructions regarding War Diaries and Intelligence Summaries are contained in F. S. Regs., Part II. and the Staff Manual respectively. Title pages will be prepared in manuscript.

Place	Date	Hour	Summary of Events and Information	Remarks and references to Appendices
	March			
MARTINPUICH	6		Two guns from A, B & D Bty were taken up to position East of MARTINPUICH.	WD WD
	7		Two 18 pdrs & 2 4.5 Hows sent to position.	WD
	8		78th Bde H.Q. went into action & took over tactical command of "KIRKESSOP" Group consisting of A, B & D batteries of 78th Bde & B, C & D batteries 79th Bde. Group guns were as follows on GREVILLERS Trench from G.32.d.6.2 to M.4.b.0.5.	65
	9		All batteries registered on GREVILLERS Trench & LOUPART Trench from G.33.6.5.6 to 53.4.d.7.0. B/78 shelled with 21 cm hostile howitzer —	WD
	10		All batteries in the Group carried out barrages as laid down in 2nd Divisional O.O. No 55 on GREVILLERS Trench at ZERO & lifting onto LOUPART trench at ZERO + 6 when a standing barrage was maintained. B/78 searched & swept LOUPART WOOD. The attack was reported successful all objectives reached & held ad alept cost — several machine guns & trench guns captured.	WD
	11		Further advances by our Infantry guns out of range. Thursday registering.	WD
	12		" " " "	WD

WAR DIARY or INTELLIGENCE SUMMARY

Army Form C. 2118.

Place	Date	Hour	Summary of Events and Information	Remarks and references to Appendices
	MARCH			
MARTIN PRICE	13th		Preparations begun for withdrawing guns from the line & handing over of ammunition 2nd Div Art.	W.D.
"	14th		Work of dumping ammunition continued.	W.D.
"	15th		Some of the guns & detachments withdrawn to wagon lines	W.D.
"	16th		Remaining guns & detachments withdrawn to wagon lines at ALBERT.	W.D.
ALBERT	17th		Brigade at W.L. in ALBERT	W.D.
" PUCHEVILLERS	18th		Brigade marched to PUCHEVILLERS. On arriving there Bde. was ordered to remain at the village pending further orders to move to SUISCHART. Rest Area cancelled.	W.D.
PUCHEVILLERS	19th		Bde. at PUCHEVILLERS	W.D.
BEAUVOIR RIVIERE	20th		Bde. marched to BEAUVOIR RIVIERE	W.D.
"	21st		Brigade in rest at "	W.D.
"	22nd		Brigade at BEAUVOIR RIVIERE - orders received to proceed to BOUBERS AREA	W.D.
"	23rd		the 24th - BEAUVOIR RIVIERE - all guns sent to I.O.M at FREVENT for overhaul.	W.D.

Army Form C. 2118.

WAR DIARY
or
INTELLIGENCE SUMMARY

(Erase heading not required.)

Instructions regarding War Diaries and Intelligence Summaries are contained in F. S. Regs., Part II. and the Staff Manual respectively. Title Pages will be prepared in manuscript.

Place	Date	Hour	Summary of Events and Information	Remarks and references to Appendices
BOUBERS	24th		Brigade left BEAUVOIR & march to BOUBERS-SUR-CANCHE	h.9.D
ST. MICHEL	25th		Brigade marched to ST. MICHEL - Came under orders of XVII Corps.	h.9.D
BRAY	26th		Brigade marched to N.L. at Camp "C" S.W. of BRAY.	h.9.D
"	27th		Work carried out by parties from each Battery at gun positions under orders from 342nd Divl. Arty. and the Brigade Ammunition Column	h.9.D
"	28		Work carried out + ammunition taken to positions - guns at I.O.M FREVENT	h.9.A
"	29		" " " " " " "	h.9.A
"	30		" " " " " " "	h.9.A
"	31		" " " " " " "	h.9.D

Ammunition expended during MARCH 1917

3768 A
3255 Ax
1526 Bx.

Casualties :- Nil

J.R.W. Lyne
Lieut R.F.A.
a/Adjt 78 F.A.B
for Lieut Col Commanding 48th F.A.B

WAR DIARY
INTELLIGENCE SUMMARY

(Erase heading not required.)

Army Form C. 2118.

17th (?) / VI / R.K.B. dr R.F.A. / VI / 22

Place	Date	Hour	Summary of Events and Information	Remarks and references to Appendices
ARRAS	APRIL 1.	—	The four batteries of the 75th went into action under the tactical administration of the 34th Divisional Group – Bde H.Qrs remained at wagon lines BRAY.	w.d.
"	2.		Batteries in action and detached from the Bde H.Qrs.	w.d.
"	3.		"	w.d.
"	4.		Preliminary bombardment to an operation for a future date. "V" day which proved to be "X" day "Y" day	w.d.
"	5.		Batteries still in action under 34th Divl Group "W" day	w.d. Zero day postponed
"	6.		" " " "	w.d.
"	7.		" " " "	w.d.
"	8.		" " " " – Zero day postponed	w.d.
"	9.		24 hrs. B.Gp. – Zero hour 5.30 am	w.d.
"	10th.		B.Gp. on 10th. Zero day – Zero hour 5.30 a.m. after Zero hour 4 hours 44 minutes of 15 Zero hours at "DEAD MANS CORNER" (G.21.b.56) ARRAS and came under orders of the 50th Inf Bde Group which was attached to the 3rd Cavalry Division. Stops lost – 3 men killed and 1 wounded while waiting at this rendez. vous. – Batteries bivouacked at Arras for the night. 78th Bde at wagon lines in Arras.	w.d.
"	11th 12th 13th 14th		B.Gp moved into the line relieving batteries of the 59th Bde R.F.A – 11th Division & came under the administration of the 3rd D.A. Bde positions S. of CAMBRAI-ARRAS road in N3C & N4C. Bde H. Qrs at cross roads THILOY (N1a) —	w.d.

2449 Wt. W14957/Mgo 750,000 1/16 J.B.C. & A. Forms/C.2118/12.

Army Form C. 2118.

WAR DIARY
or
INTELLIGENCE SUMMARY
(Erase heading not required.)

Instructions regarding War Diaries and Intelligence Summaries are contained in F. S. Regs., Part II. and the Staff Manual respectively. Title Pages will be prepared in manuscript.

Place	Date	Hour	Summary of Events and Information	Remarks and references to Appendices
MONCHY	13th	—	Batteries carried out registration and calibration tests on various zones — wiring covered by the Bde N18 C 82 – 07 C 1.0. At 3.15 p.m. an attack was made on GUEMAPPE by the 9th K. Inf/Bde – 78th Bde to put up western barrage from N18 & 54 to N18 central.	W.D.
"	14th	—	No firing by 18th Bde batteries beyond usual calibration – 9.5 Hours fired 2 rounds per hr.	W.D.
"	15th	—	Throughout the day no firing O.19.a 0.7. L – O.19.a 4.9. 78th Bde. left B.2 D.A. & came under the administration of the 17 D.A. & covered 17th Div. Inf. in the line – 3.0.3 lives / 32C40 – 131a63.	W.D.
"	16th	—	A/78 moved to new position in N.4.b 46.40 – Batteries carried out registration on KEELING COPSE & Hostile artillery very active – Batteries shelled continuous by 4.7 & 77 m.m. 14.2 on + 5.9 guns + howitzers. H.E.B.4 opened fire on their S.O.S. lines in response to an S.O.S. call – fire reported effective.	W.D.
"	17th	—	Further registration on KEELING COPSE – Bois des AUBEPINES by batteries – Batteries subjected to a very continuous searching + sweeping fire during the night of 16/17 + during the day with every calibre of shell up to 21 cm. Round Cloudy & gusty wind – 1.O.R. D/78 wounded, 1.O.R. 876 slightly wounded. A certain amount of gas shell used on A/78. Visibility very bad & accurate shooting difficult. Infantry report a hostile 77 m.m. gun sniping their trenches at H.28.c stunning direction of fire	W.D.
"	18th	—	"CHEMICAL WORKS" & KEELING COPSE & CROSSROADS checked by batteries – Batteries still being heavily shelled during day & night – position becoming untenable at times & had to be evacuated. Trip shelling heavy — CAMBRAI ROAD in vicinity of batteries continually under barrage. Rendering supply of ammunition difficult – Enemy suspected shell fall — on observer with B/78 of A/78 in MONCHY on some such suitable point of observation to new position M.3407.6 under heavy shellfire – Batteries heavily shelled 1/73. Enemy 1.25 a. registered – calibration. 1 wounded. Officer shot, shell hit on gun — 3 men killed 1 wounded. Visibility low. Enemy still suspected of having observer in our lines.	W.D.
"	19th	—		W.D.

2449 Wt. W14957/M90 750,000 1/16 J.B.C. & A. Forms/C.2118/12.

WAR DIARY or INTELLIGENCE SUMMARY

Army Form C. 2118.

Place	Date	Hour	Summary of Events and Information	Remarks and references to Appendices
MONCHY	20th		All Bty fired on S.O.S Lines previous night 8.30 p.m. until enemy barrage was located & continued more front N. of R.S. CARTER. D/78 fired on active hostile battery at 2.16 p.m. in J.27.C. - it was an aerial target. Batteries have checked as nearly Visibility fair. - Our planes very active. - 97F moved to new position at N.34.d.5.6.	W.D.
"	21st		Our fire directed - 18 Pdr harassing fire by day on neighbourhood in Div.S. front west of grid running through EAST and D/KESLING C.B.P3.E. rounds fired throughout the day. Harasst. fire of CAMBRAI and hostile battery positions - hostile front line over TWIGG'S PIT. Aerial activity intermittent. Some normal. Two hostile planes flew over TWIGG'S PIT. Enemy at low altitude + were engaged by our A.A. + disappeared After D.H. fired on hostile active battery in response to our call from the Lin.	W.D.
"	22nd		All batteries kept up continual harassing fire on enemy shown on Photos as heavy day. Barrage times as twilight on morning of 23rd + front line fortifications. Several aeroplanes were called down by A/78 D/78 & D/76. Hostile submarines - Visibility good.	W.D.
"	23rd		Barrage fire carried out by all Btys on enemy front line & support in N.7.D.A.O.9 N.7576 - Zero hour 4.45 a.m. - attack having arranged. All batteries went over - during afternoon MONCHY & ORANGE HILL heavily shelled. Two hostile aeroplanes were knocked out by dead - hit - the other came back - apparently having crossed the coast. The attack before Infantry was ready on Consequently artillery killed ineffective. - Enemy planes brought down west of MONCHY on south of CAMBRAI road. - All 5.30 p.m. all batteries carried out bombardment as ordered; to which our artillery replied with stop shelled activity. Damaged our front & batteries very active during the night - heavily barraged on S.O.S reported the enemy were massing in BOIRY NOTRE DAME. - Visibility good.	W.D.
"	24th		On this whole a quiet day - an artillery carried out fire registration on KESLING COPSE + also fired in accordance with order J.34 carried out down in ≠ 17. D.A.BM/119. on RIFLE TRENCH. Party of enemy seen entering area J.34 central fired on by H/78 with M.H.E. - good results were obtained Protective Barrage carried out this morning commencing at 3.40 over RIFLE TRENCH at ordered by W.O. No. 3. 24/4/117. Steady pale Parties kept up Knoops Pit the day on FUZE TRENCH, SHELL TRENCH and CARTRIDGE TRENCH. Hostile Artillery on normal. Big explosion seen in enemy lines	W.D.
"	25th		Visibility good. ZERO HOUR 3.20 a.m.	W.D.

WAR DIARY or INTELLIGENCE SUMMARY

Army Form C. 2118

Place	Date	Hour	Summary of Events and Information	Remarks and references to Appendices
MONCHY	26.		Party of enemy in I.34.D fired at - shell burst amongst them disappeared into a trench. No S.L. firing on ponds and valleys behind S.O.S. lines (I.32.D.04 to I.32.A.11) as ordered. Hostile fire less normal. Intermittent shelling by Enemy of N5d, N5c, b, 5d and 24.2. Visibility good. Hostile balloons up daytime brought down - planes by our aircraft. Big explosion in trenches of ours, behind enemy lines about 1 P.M.	R.T.
"	27.		Two S.O.S. calls responded to Batteries at 9 p.m. + 4.30 a.m. No S.O.S. Red celling gone up from own Infantry and mistake evidently due to similarity with Very gain used by enemy. Several aeroplane calls answered by A/78 on I.32, G.2.8. Hostile fire less normal. 50 R. C.B.R. shells exploded at 8/78 position (N.3.C.7.5) destroyed by shell fire. Visibility fair. At 11.30a.m. a new crater was seen to go up in direction of BOIS-DES-AUBÉPINES and at 11.45 a.m. a new crater to go up in direction of O.16.	R.T.
"	28.		At 4.45 a.m. this morning ZERO HOUR - all batteries of Divisional Artillery Group carried out barrage as laid down in 12 K. Div. Artilly. O.O. No. 30 dated 27/4/17. During the morning calibration and corrections checked on I.25, d, 7, 5. All batteries fired on protective barrage lines and zeroed valleys in I.32 a & c and I.26, c, t, d, as ordered. Batteries fired on S.O.S. lines at 9 P.M. and 11 P.m. in response to signals which were eventually found to be of Rozhe origin. Area of Battery positions swept by hostile artillery bombardment and A/78 had 10.R. killed and 5 O.R. wounded. During the morning three of our contact planes were fired in turn - a BEEF and a RED C as a result. Machine Gun fire from ROEUX - landed at H.29, a, 7, 8 and H.29, G, 8, 5 respectively. Another BEEF Lewis forced to land SW of TIGSAW WOOD as the result of combat with an ALBATROSS Scout.	R.T.
"	29.		Night firing as per 12 Kav. Arty. O.O. R.7/4 & 28/4/17. Relief of RIFLE TRENCH occupied by enemy shelled continuously by our Artillery. A/78 fired on KEELING COPSE - a number of the enemy lying in open about I.27.c engaged with shrapnel and knocked out. Enemy artillery very active around Battery positions - repeated bursts of fire at short intervals with 4.2 cm, 15 cm, & 21 cm. How.	R.T.

WAR DIARY or INTELLIGENCE SUMMARY

Army Form C. 2118

Place	Date	Hour	Summary of Events and Information	Remarks and references to Appendices
PONCHY	29 (cont.)		from following directions:- 29° E of Thushy Tower from position at N.41.B, 40,40, from about Railway Cutting H.15.a, and End ground H.15.B, 80.16. also from H.15.a+b. +I.25.+I.29.a. Visibility:- O.P. suspected at I, 1 H 7. B, 5, 5. Small parties of enemy in trench running from I.25.C,7,2 + I.25.C,9,1, effectively engaged by C/78. Law of our planes brought down -and on flames + the other punched about 200 yds in front of C/78 O.P. at I.23.d,13. His'd party carried out as ordered + all hacks, shrubs + approaches etc in Bde zone. From 3+1 a.m. (Zero hour) to 4+1 a.m. Barrages were carried out as laid down by 37th Divs Bde order of 29/4/17. All batteries carried out further protective barrage on S.O.S. line in reply to enemy counter-attack. During the day continuous fire maintained on trench I.32, a,b,c,d. + I.32.c,d,+ as requested by Infantry. Hostile fire above normal - very active thoughout day + + neighbourhood of battery positions until 2.1 a.m. 15" gun 10.5" + 7.2" about I.2,B,12,40. Snowstorm during the forenoon. About 12-10 pm enemy planes observed. Visibility poor during afternoon. About 3 pm an HL BATTERY (about ?ones) + (ano + machine gun fire) in valley approximately I.33.B,B,b.	P.T. fit
"	30"			fit

AMMUNITION EXPENDED DURING APRIL 1917:-

14,469 A.
8,667 A.X.
80/3 B.X.
114 B @ B.R.
300 B.S.K.

Casualties:- N.O.R.
Killed:- 1 O.R.
Wounded:- 1 Officer + 29 O.R.

P.T. Nott, 2nd Lt. R.F.A.
for Lieut Col Commanding
78th F.A.B.

Vol 23
78th BRIGADE, R.F.A.

WAR DIARY or INTELLIGENCE SUMMARY

(Erase heading not required.) Army Form C. 2118

MAY 1917

Place	Date MAY	Hour	Summary of Events and Information	Remarks and references to Appendices
MONCHY	1.		All Batteries carried out Barrages from 4 a.m. to 4.8 a.m. as ordered in 12th D.A.O.O. No. 33. At 12.55 p.m. 2 p.m. and 3.15 p.m. 78 position vicinity of FEUCHY CHAPEL subjected to concentrated bombardment with 15 c.m. Hows. Visibility good. Hostile aeroplanes over Battery positions. Heavy Hostile Barrage on our front line.	R.7.
"	2.		Batteries carried out Barrages from 1 a.m. as ordered mid-noon day-night firing. At 12.20 a.m. heavy enemy bombardment of four Zones. At 12.25 a.m. F.O.P. signals reported by F.O.O. and our guns opened fire. At 1.50 a.m. all quiet on our front. Heavy Hostile shelling with 8" & 5.9" F.G. CAMBRAI ROAD and west-bound of N36. About 1200 rounds fell in the neighbourhood during last 24 hours. Visibility poor at first, but improved. Enemy seen in I 26 c.	B.7.
"	3.		Bombardment with chemical shell carried out by 4.5" Hows from 8.30 p.m. onwards as per 12 R.F.A. O.O. No. 35. Salvoes by 4.5" each hour on HATCHET WOOD. All Batteries carried out Barrages from ZERO HOUR (3.45 a.m.) as ordered in 12 R.F.A. O.O. 34. an attack being made by our Infantry. Enemy promptly counter attacked but were stopped by Machine Gunfire Artillery Barrage suffering very heavy casualties. Visibility poor in early hours but improved. No flying Planes. No movement in KEELING COPSE but our Infantry be seen forming behind in front of SCABBARD TRENCH. Enemy aircraft very active.	R.7.
"	4.		Nise. firing on roads & approaches in Bela Zone. GUN and CARTRIDGE TRENCHES kept under continual bursts of fire during the day. Aeroplane target 0,9,a,2, fired at 3 p.m. by A/78. Hostile movement - nil. Enemy placing Balow normal - some enemy smoothle fire in vicinity of CAMBRAI ROAD towards TILLOY. Visibility fair.	B.7.

WAR DIARY
or
INTELLIGENCE SUMMARY.
(Erase heading not required.)

Army Form C. 2118.

Place	Date	Hour	Summary of Events and Information	Remarks and references to Appendices
MONCHY	May 5		Night firing carried out and GUN & CARTRIDGE TRENCHES kept under fire during the day. Hostile activity less normal – a few gas shells fell in vicinity of A/78 position. Silent sniper posts by enemy seen about I.28,c,17,0 moving to PARK WORK, I.17.S.W. WOOD and behind BOIS DU SART. Visibility poor.	BZ
"	6.		Night firing carried out beyond S.O.S. lines. Snipers during day & parties present from I.17.S.W. WOOD to SANDPIT LANE I.27.D.30.40. Hostile fire below normal, area round I.31.W. CHAPELLE shelled during day with 7.7 guns. Enemy aircraft energetic. Visibility fair. Quiet on our front.	BZ
"	7.		Night firing as ordered on GUN TRENCH in I.32.A. Calibration carried out during day. Heavy hostile fire on battery positions in N.5.D and N.6.c by 5.9 in the morning. Visibility good. One of our planes crashed by him red devils in H.12.d. at 4.30 a.m. Both carried on as day out.	BZ
"	8.		Night firing as ordered & approaches south of 3.O.S. lines. Hostile fire between 11 p.m. + 12 midnight at enemy gas shelled railway – H.35.b. and also shelled H.33 at intervals. Knocking day. Visibility poor. Quiet on our front.	BZ
"	9.		N.S. firing carried out as ordered. Rpts D/A/78 position heavily shelled during the day out 4.2. + 7.7 cms. FEUCHY CHAPELLE corner area shelled 7.9 + 9 off an all day. Visibility good. Aeroplane dropped down by enemy Red Devils in H.18.A. pilot wounded. Prisoner apparently uninjured,	BZ
"	10.		Night firing as ordered. Calibration on DEVIL'S TRENCH and CARTRIDGE TRENCH checked, satisfactory. Misfiring no orders. During night several gas shells and 4.2 chappers – south S/78 position. 8 found in FEUCHY CHAPELLE corner at 2.30 p.m. New sniper ind: L8/178/L. cist.n. H.33.B. + d, H.34. a. &c. Visibility good. Hostile Gun at Heavy Cal. Bn fired on MONCHY, Shrapnel fired from I.18,a,2,1, Grande Battery opened + dump can be go up.	BZ

WAR DIARY
or
INTELLIGENCE SUMMARY.
(Erase heading not required.)

Army Form C. 2118.

Place	Date MAY	Hour	Summary of Events and Information	Remarks and references to Appendices
MONCHY	10.		Night quiet as ordered. SPIDER and CARTRIDGE TRENCH bombarded 9.45 to 10 p.m. Hostile activity below normal. Visibility low owing to slight haze.	B.I.
	11.		DEVIL and ANGEL TRENCHES reached in accordance with I.A.O. & O. No 37 areas opened with attack by 4. K.R.A.	(B.I)
	12.		ANGEL TRENCH, GRENADE TRENCH and SUN TRENCH Bombarded at 6.30 a.m. in accordance with I.A. O. No. 37. at pm Standing Barrage in CENTRE TRENCH and STWELL TRENCH bombarded in I.A. O. No 38 — 25th Divn Canadians making an attack on DEVIL TRENCH	(B.I)
				B.I
	14.		Nothing carried out — also Barrage during day as ordered. Approaches to Role. 20 N.E. reported. During night enemy placed B/I's position with 4.2". Enemy retaliated bombardment by barrage on front line MONCHY Ravil. Visibility fair. Enemy sent up Garden Rain Rockets from D 31.16. TRENCH at commencement of our Barrage. Hostile aircraft active.	B.I
	15.		Nothing carried out on points heavily rack areas. Calibration checked. Heavy enemy shelling included all day. North side of the river SCARPE especially from about ROEUX. Visibility, ROEUX shelled with 5-9 h. Visibility good.	B.I.
	16.		Night looks carried out as ordered & calibrations checked. Heavy hostile fire in early morning in H 34.1 C & D. H 28 C & D with 7.7 cm, 4.5 cm Hows. Heavy fire also on ROEUX. Visibility good. Enemy movement nil — no hostile balloons observed.	B.I

Army Form C. 2118.

Instructions regarding War Diaries and Intelligence Summaries are contained in F. S. Regs., Part II. and the Staff Manual respectively. Title pages will be prepared in manuscript.

WAR DIARY
or
INTELLIGENCE SUMMARY.
(Erase heading not required.)

Place	Date May	Hour	Summary of Events and Information	Remarks and references to Appendices
MONCHY	17.		The 7th today fairly as usual. Hostile fire practically nil - a few 4.2 on front line, 11.30 and N12. Hostile b/g very poor - no enemy increased shering. At 5 p.m. to-day 9.B.2 & R.G.A. S.A.A. overcame.	B.I 1
"	18.		No firing on our shorts reported or observed. Hostile shering of MENCHY & N.W.A. nil 10.5 and 15 cm. from direction of PLOUVAIN. Enemy aircraft active over battery positions. Visibility good.	B.I 1
"	19.		Calibration during day. T.W.O. and Dr. Nr6 TRENCH bombed. Heavy rifle shelling of H25C, H3H, B3 15cm. + 10cm. shers. Enemy movement in PICCADILLY TRENCH. Aeroplane observation. Enfilade balloons burnt. One from RE.2 & planes brought down 3 German planes at 7 p.m. One German plane shot down + 2 injured bought by our planes at 8 A.M.	B.I 1
"	20.		2nd C.O. 72 converted. BOIS DU SART and on N46 O4 TRENCH bombed. Heavy rifle fire, N3L, B4 4.5" Hors fired on O4 O+O4D. Enemy shelled N5A on N75 and crossroads at N3L by 4.5" Hors during the morning. Enemy unlucky posts seen in BOIRY TRENCH & dispersed by our 4.5" Hors. At 11.30 a.m. 4 RED devils attacked our 5pm control machine which 3 drove up slowly + damped down one of the enemy / red - devils while caged on our line making practice. Visibility poor.	B.I 1
"	21.		Machine gun tactical shoots appended to programme T.O.C. less as ordered. Discomfort by enemy battery on H27C H22C H22C+H22C. Whole day very fine. Hostile aircraft very active. Enemy aeroplane flying low over front line & battery positions. Panche battery 5/16 shots. Balloons active.	B.I 1
"	22.		O17B on S5730 + 1 TRENCH with 90 rounds. Next day & to hand. Hostile fire & 1 binocular. B.I Visibility poor. Payrolls running taken P. Pres - Morris bulletins.	B.I 1

WAR DIARY or INTELLIGENCE SUMMARY

Army Form C. 2118.

Place	Date May	Hour	Summary of Events and Information	Remarks and references to Appendices
MONCHY	23.		Missing & wounded. Retaliation at 1 p.m. as ordered. Hostile Shelling of H32.C. 9.30 p.m. to 10.30 p.m. by H.V. Velocity 4.1. Visibility good. Quiet day.	R.Z.
"	24.		Nightfiring harassing tasks carried out as ordered. B.O.I.R / T.RENCH engaged by Hostile Battery. Hostile fire below normal and quiet. Visibility good. At 8 a.m. one of our planes brought down a fire landing South of N.10 N.4. Movement round PARK WOOD. Stable fellows seen from O/P N.8. O.P. Keenings taken. A.P's complete round O.P. at 70 N.4 H.	R.Z.
"	25.		C/78 carried out special wire cutting task at junct. of DEVILS TRENCH and BIT LANE. C/78 carried out special wire cutting task at 6.20 a.m. 150 rounds fired no ordered 25 R.F.A. B/78 on Counter Preparation lines of N5 and S. Tank of N10 N.4 H/Ey 10 Gun. and 15 Cun. Visibility intermittent. Hostile fire of N5 and S. Tank of N10 N.4 H/Ey 10 Gun. and 15 Cun. Visibility good. Hostile aircraft active our Battery positions and N32.B.	R.Z.
"	26.		Batteries checked new datum points at O.P. Quiver. Hostile fire above normal. Harassing fire by enemy Staffs on trencher tracks & Battery positions in N4, N5, H32 H33 H34. Visibility good. One of our planes forced landed in H36 at about 7.30 p.m. Enemy aircraft active.	B7
"	27.		Nil.t & anything no normal. Hostile fire below normal. Visibility good. Hostile aircraft active.	B7
"	28.		Nightfiring carried out as ordered in 29 Div Artey Instructions No.227 - at 3.0 A. Nightfiring carried out today. Fair to fair effects seen from O.P. 18 Patrol engaged Batteries 22.S carried out Gas Work, Hostile shelling of N4, D, F, G, with 15 cm howitzer. PUPPY TRENCH and BEER WORK. Hostile shelling of N4, D, F, G, with 15 cm howitzer. E36 Visibility good. Eny brought down cast of HOOK and LONG TRENCH enemy seen to leave	R.Z.

WAR DIARY
or
INTELLIGENCE SUMMARY.

Army Form C. 2118.

Place	Date	Hour	Summary of Events and Information	Remarks and references to Appendices
MONCHY	MAY 29.		How Battery carried out bombardment of HOOK and LONG TRENCHES. Signal cables by 18 Pdrs. 100 yards beyond S.O.S. during night arranged. Batteries - N 4 & 8 bombarded by Enemy throughout to-day - N 5 B + D, N 6 a + c also observed flashes by 5.9. Nothing good. Some shearing taken from O.P. N 12, 6, 50, & 2 & 4 enemy guns in position.	(37)
"	30.		HOOK and LONG TRENCHES Bombarded by How. as on previous day. 18 Pdrs kept up harassing fire on POPPY TRENCH and GREEN WOOD. Enemy retaliated by light trench mortars chiefly about the night on area found in vicinity of SHRAPNEL TRENCH 10.4.5pm 6-7.30am. Intermittent Rifle Sniper during day of MONCHY, N 5, 6, and N 5, d, and 7, 7 and 70.5 sec. Nothing significant. Enemy otherwise quiet.	(13)
"	31.		Operations and registration carried out in accordance with 23 L Bn O.O. No 74 received. Infantry working on WORK on HOOK TRENCH during day were engaged how & LONG TRENCHES and 18 Pdrs. on COUNTER PREPARATION LINE as arranged. Intercept labour during which 5 good during quiet day.	(9P)

AMMUNITION EXPENDED DURING MAY 1917.

14,845 A.
12,264 A.X.
9,872 Bx.
182 BSK.
452 BCaR.

CASUALTIES :-

KILLED :- 2 O.R.
WOUNDED :- 2 Officers + 15 O.R.

R. Talbot, Lt. RFA
Adjt. 78 Bde. RFA
for Lt Col Commanding 78 Bde RFA

Army Form C. 2118.

WAR DIARY
or
INTELLIGENCE SUMMARY.

(Erase heading not required.)

WO 24 78th BRIGADE, R.F.A.

JUNE 1917

Place	Date	Hour	Summary of Events and Information	Remarks and references to Appendices
MONCHY	1.	10 a.m.	5 minutes intense fire in BOIS DU VERT. Usual harassing shoots. Hows. bombarded LONE TRENCH 18 Febr.ges. on GREEN WORK and DEVIL'S TRENCH during bombardment by Heavies. 8178 pivoted 3 Kite Balloon on N.E. corner of BOIS DU VERT. Enemy shelled N6c and N11c at intervals. Enemy aircraft very active. Observe enemy movement practically nil. Wachtlof good.	R.F.
"	2.		Usual harassing shoots carried out - GREEN WORK, PUPPY TRENCH and LONE TRENCH engaged. Enemy apparently shelled N4 and C17c Ballaycoorter with 5.9 and 6.1 from direction of PELVES. 3 O.P.'s put out of action fire at B176 position. No hostile aircraft active along our front. Wachtlof good.	R.F.
"	3.		Usual harassing shoots carried out as ordered. Enemy fire below normal. Wachtlof good.	R.F.
"	4.		Usual aircraft day harassing shoots. Very little enemy movement. Wachtlof fair.	R.F.
"	5.		Usual day harassing shoots. GREEN WORK regd. with Balloon 8mentor. Enemy fire below normal. Wachtlof good. Enemy movement nil.	R.F.
"	6.		Harassing as usual. Enemy shelled H34 & V434 at mt. 5.9 during the evening also N12c and O7 J6 and 10.15 4.15 a.m. N12L also shelled with 8 cm. YELLOW WOOD with 5.9." and Enemy aircraft active from B-his plains flying low over Battery positions. Hostile plane shot down (3 Neuport) in BOIS DE BOEUF. One of our Neuports also crashed head on Monchy. Hostile Battery O.B.10 reported by aeroplane engaged by 8.178, B.173. Moved to new position. Wachtlof poor.	R.F.
"	7.	10.10 p.m. to 10.20 p.m.	SOS. Lines B, Z etc., ordered. Heavy hostile barrage on N.12 and N.12c G 5.5.G. Throughout the day, Wachtlof and enemy movement active during day on our front. Pensles.	R.F.

A 583.4 W.T. W.973-M.687. 750,000 8/16 D.D. & L. Ltd. Forms/C.2118/13.

WAR DIARY
or
INTELLIGENCE SUMMARY.

Army Form C. 2118.

Place	Date	Hour	Summary of Events and Information	Remarks and references to Appendices
MONCHY	8.		Harassing fire as detailed in S.O.74 O.O No I. Hostile fire normal. N6 emplaced at intervals at noon. 6 of Hr enemy came into trenches at O8 central surrendered. Visibility good.	B.7.
"	9.		Night & day continuous harassing fire as ordered. Hostile fire probably nil. Visibility poor. Enemy aeroplane active during morning.	B.7.
"	10.		Night & day fire as ordered. Retaliation checked. Enemy placed N5 at intervals during whole day with it 12 and 5.50. Visibility poor. Quiet day.	B.7.
"	11.		Barrage firing as ordered. 9 Tree Trench 11pm to 3am night 10th/11th. Chemical shell fired on enemy's batteries & trenches. Filling battery area. Methane gas shells picked up near Telegraph hill followed by every possible retaliation. [illegible] 12 noon to 1 pm Trench mortar & gas shell put into enemy's trenches & batteries with Chemical Shell reply 5.50. Visibility poor.	R.PR.7. B.7.
"	12		Day and night harassing fire and bombardment 3 Hos. Batteries and Chemical Shell as ordered. Enemy placed enemy 1 OB9 with 77 mm Trench mortars 3 B0 & B5 Vert East 9 Trench repaired intermittently. H.V. H.E. Gunfire fired women at 4.34 & central. Visibility poor during morning increasing in afternoon. Enemy fell shell near Bois de Aubespines at 11.15am. 3 aeroplanes.	B.7.
"	13.		Harassing firing 5 18Pdr and Bombardment of Hos. Batteries with HE as ordered. Registration carried out. Enemy placed N4 during night with 77 cm. Hostile Balloon firing on Hussar and Vine Trenches during morning. Visibility fair.	B.7.

WAR DIARY
or
INTELLIGENCE SUMMARY.
(Erase heading not required.)

Army Form C. 2118.

Place	Date	Hour	Summary of Events and Information	Remarks and references to Appendices
MONCHY	14		Hostile m.g. firing by 16 Pdrs. & Bombardment by Howr. with H.E. as ordered. 17 K.O.A Group carried out Barrage (Zero Hour 7.20 a.m.) as ordered by 2nd D.A. O.P. No 3 due 17/6/17 & spot up during day in accordance with programme from Officers Infantry Bde. H.R. & Puppy Trench and Southern end of Bois du Vert. Enemy in reply to our barrage opened rapidly in morning of bombardment & our howitzers. Heavy enemy fire on Monchy, all batteries up to 5.9. Visibility good.	BZ.
	15		At 5.30 pm (appx.17) opened an S.O.S. lines in reply to Infantry S.O.S. rockets on our line & bombardment signal. At 7.30pm S.O.S. went on Sunray trench area. At 9.35pm. An S.O.S. lines for our ground in reply to call from Infantry Bde. Hows. two opened fire as ordered. N 5 & N 10 shelled in morning. At 8.25pm three Nieuports shot down two German planes	BZ.
ARRAS	16		Batteries of 78th Bde. R.F.A. withdrew to wagon lines. S.E.C. (51 B.N.W. map). 76th Bde. R.F.A. marched to new wagon lines.	RZ.
			Batteries of 78 & 74 Bde. R.F.A. went into position (relieved by 51st F.A.B.) on night 16/17 & June. B/78, C/78, D/78, Capt. over positions A/78, thus making new positions. (H 9 b + c & L 2, 4, 3, 9, 2, 8). Map 51 B. N.W.) Under command of C.R.A. left Divisional Artillery XVII Corps.	
GAVRELLE	17		Came into action and registered S.O.S. lines. Work on gun pits, ammunition pits, O.P.'s began.	BZ.
PLOUVAIN	18		Harrassing Bombardments and searching places to N. was ordered by 24 D.A. O.O. No 9 S.C. Hostile aircraft active. Hostile fire on Battery & works retaliated or my fire	BZ.
	19		Harrassing fire as ordered. Chemical Shell Bombardment as ordered. H 10 shelled Punjab at night with gas shells.	BZ.
	20		Harrassing fire as ordered. Quiet day.	BZ.

Army Form C. 2118.

WAR DIARY
or
INTELLIGENCE SUMMARY.
(Erase heading not required.)

Instructions regarding War Diaries and Intelligence Summaries are contained in F.S. Regs., Part II. and the Staff Manual respectively. Title pages will be prepared in manuscript.

Place	Date June	Hour	Summary of Events and Information	Remarks and references to Appendices
GAVRELLE - PLOUVAIN	21.		Harassing fire carried out as ordered in Sq. K.94.00.98. Enemy shelled Hq & at intervals and also fired at intervals between 9 a.m. & 2.30 a.m. with 8 inch Hows at vicinity of Point du Jour R. Habit Gain.	B.Z.
	22.		Harassing fire continued as ordered. Chemical works shelled with 77 mm at intervals. 1 A.H. shell with 4.2" Howitzer. Gas mine commenced 2.17am & at 10 a.m. Harassing fire & Bombardment by How. Battery as ordered.	B.Z.
	23.			B.Z.
	24.		Harassing fire carried out as ordered. Enemy shelled Point du Jour & H.100 during morning & also shelled Hq. & with 10 a.m. 6/5 cm. guns rate of fire several rounds per minute. Several Hostile Batteries located by flash & sound.	B.Z.
	25.		Harassing fire as ordered. Enemy shelled Pont du Jour throughout the day. also 17c in retaliation to our Bombardment. Hostile O.P.s & Travel Tellung located & Excessive Hits obtained by Battery. Hostile Infantry moving from close to our lines retaliated by field batteries.	B.Z.
	26.		Bombardment carried out as ordered. Calibration checked. Hostile fire below normal. Quiet day.	B.Z.
	27.		Barrage on WIT TREVOR carried out at 1.01 a.m. Hostile fire below normal. Hostile Guns - no unusual movement. Registration carried out.	B.Z.

Army Form C. 2118.

WAR DIARY
or
INTELLIGENCE SUMMARY.
(Erase heading not required.)

Place	Date June	Hour	Summary of Events and Information	Remarks and references to Appendices
SAVREUSE	28.		Calibration carried out. Bombardment carried out at Zero Hour 7-10 p.m. as ordered by 17 K.O.A.O./No.81 in co-operation with attack by 31st Division on our left. SAVREUSE MILL PONT DU ROAD pieces extensively. By 77 c.m. gun in rear of our Bombardment. Heavy Machine Gun fire from Left from at WINDMILL and RAILWAY EMBANKMENT. Enemy Barrage very thin and did not cause any appreciable reply to our Bombardment.	R.2
"	29.		Harassing fire carried out in accordance with programme Bombardment by 6.0/78 with Gas Shell on Cow Trench as ordered by 17 K.O.A.O.O. No.82. Hostile artillery seemed to slack.	R.2
"	30.		My Works - peaceably place holes - carried out by 181 Bde. as ordered by 17 K.O.A.O.O. No. 83. Enemy fire over all below normal. Visibility poor. Work on new pits, ammunition pits &c. continues.	R.2

AMMUNITION EXPENDED DURING JUNE 1917.-
10,929 A.
8,975 A X.
5,850 B X.
826 B.E.B.R.
75 B.S.K.

CASUALTIES:-
WOUNDED: 1 Officer
4 O.R.

R. Torlett
2/Lieut R.F.A.
A/Adjt. 78th Bde R.F.A.
for O.C. 78th Bde R.F.A.

WAR DIARY
or
INTELLIGENCE SUMMARY.
(Erase heading not required.)

Army Form C. 2118.

VII 2 78th BRIGADE, R.F.A.

Summary of Events and Information — July 1917

REF: TRENCH MAP: FRANCE 51 B.N.W. 1:20,000.

Place	Date July	Hour	Summary of Events and Information	Remarks and references to Appendices
GAVRELLE ROEUX PLOUVAIN	1.		Night firing programme carried out as ordered. Enemy fire practically nil.	A.
"	2.		Harassing fire on enemy houses, track areas. Enemy shelled GAVRELLE H.Q.'s and POINT-DU-JOUR at intervals with 77cm. + 5.9 during the day. 776 engd. by Hostile Battery V16 hof-7900.	B.
"	3.		Harassing fire period at according to programme. New trench in I.3 fired on 776 had during the day + 16 Poh's during the night. Trench motor reported active from WHIP TRENCH engd. by 776.	C.
"	4.		Hostile trench motor reports active at 3 a.m. engd. by Hows. and silenced at 7.15 a.m. Enemy shelled CONRAD and COL IN TRENCHES in I.31 A+B.	D.
"	5.		Harassing fire carried out. Enemy shelled H.Q.'s and C. with 5.9 during the morning. Poh's + Batteries during practices nil.	E.
"	6.		Harassing fire carried out. Enemy movement practically nil.	F.
"	7.			
"	8.		Continuing fire during night on WHIP CROSS ROADS to silence hostile machine guns. Enemy retaliated with 4.2 How's on PONT DU JOUR.	G.
"	9.		Fire rather normal - quiet day.	H.
"	10.		Harassing fire carried out. During the night enemy shell broke over an H.E. salt 4.1 (HE) gun.	I.
"	11.		Destructive shoot on WIBBLE TRENCH carried out with good results. Hostile 776 achieving neuts. Near battery reported at WHIP CROSS ROADS successfully.	J.

Army Form C. 2118.

WAR DIARY
or
INTELLIGENCE SUMMARY.

(Erase heading not required.) 78th BRIGADE R.F.A.

July 1917

Instructions regarding War Diaries and Intelligence Summaries are contained in F.S. Regs., Part II. and the Staff Manual respectively. Title pages will be prepared in manuscript.

Place	Date	Hour	Summary of Events and Information	Remarks and references to Appendices
GAVRELLE	12.		From 5 pm. to 7 pm. area round H9c shelled at intervals of 10 minutes. 4.2". and 5.9" from 7pm to 11 pm. B3 4.2" and 5.9".	B.7.
	13.		878 arrival and one out of MAT TRENCH with 40 rounds last also shelled T.T.6 at 8.50 pm. 12.15 a.m. and 2.50 a.m. Enemy barrage C15 + CM141 TRENCHES then about 150 of the enemy raided our Bombing post E8 across from CUTHBERT TRENCH and NE of Batteries fired on S.O.S. lines at 12.8 a.m.	B.7.
	14.		Through 14/15 raid carried out R WIT TRENCH with rounds WIT and NOBBLE TRENCHES Barrage B our guns on lines B3 17 and OO 92.	B.7.
	15.		Enemy placed 5 FO.N.T. on TOUR with 4.2 Hows. during the morning.	B.
	16.		SOS flash fired by all Batteries in response to request from fort for rounds. Hostile belts barrage. At 4.30 a.m. C.O. at COGBURN TRENCH observed 7.7 ours. at 6.45 a.m. Brickworks in I.7a. shelled with 4.2 a.m. 4 pm. shells 8. GLOSTER WOOD. Came about P. blacks normal.	B.
	17.		At 11 a.m. T.N. about 2.6.77 fired on 6 Hows. with good effect. 06 7 a.m. enemy shelled FAMPOUR with 5.9 Hows. 12.15 pm. 4.2 a.m. Hos fired on the road H17.B, from the S.W. edge of GLOSTER WOOD	B.
	18.		Hostile fire normal. Enemy shelled H9A and B during the afternoon with 7.7 ours. T.T.6 active during night. Enemy gas detachments fairly on 4.2 Hows. periodically.	B.

Army Form C. 2118.

WAR DIARY
or
INTELLIGENCE SUMMARY.
(Erase heading not required.)

July 1917   75th BRIGADE R.F.A.

Place	Date July	Hour	Summary of Events and Information	Remarks and references to Appendices
GAVRELLE	19th		Harassing fire carried out. During the night enemy placed CUTHBERT with 5.9 How. at 3.45 pm. Put a slight barrage on our front line for 5 minutes. Critical work to CUTH TRENCH.	G.
"	20th	2.17 pm	Brigade fired 3 rounds Gunfire at WHP, Cross Roads, NWC TRENCH and SQUARE WOOD. Enemy active. Hostile shrapnel. Wire cutting carried out B.How. reported 3 infants trying to repair gap.	R.T.
"	21st		Harassing fire as per programme. During night enemy placed PONT du JOUR ROAD and HQ.10 with shrapnel. Between 11 a.m. to noon enemy fired several rounds 4.2 at our buns at HQ 6 & RQ 13 afterwards shelled C/75 Battery position with 4.20 & 5.9 C.I.	R.T.
"	22		Celebration carried out. Hostile fire very active. C/75 & D/75 battery position shelled. 4.20 in yesterdays at intervals of 1 to 5 mins during the entire day. Opened 3 bursts from direction of WTTREP. Many hostile aeroplanes over battery positions during morning. At 11 entry. Observation balloon taken.	B.T.
"	23		Night fire carried at as per order. Hostile fire practically nil. Hostile fire quieter than front.	R.T.
"	24th		Harassing fire as per programme. Retaliation carried out. Between 10 pm & 1 a.m. enemy two gun shells & neighbourhood of C/75 Battery position. Enemy shelled I.13.d and I.14.c Between 5 a.m. to 6 a.m. with three 5.9 shells. Enemy aircraft active.	R.T.

Army Form C. 2118.

WAR DIARY
or
INTELLIGENCE SUMMARY.
(Erase heading not required.)

78th Brigade R.F.A. July

Instructions regarding War Diaries and Intelligence Summaries are contained in F.S. Regs., Part II. and the Staff Manual respectively. Title pages will be prepared in manuscript.

Place	Date July	Hour	Summary of Events and Information	Remarks and references to Appendices
GAVRELLE	25		Calibration carried out. Enemy shelled S.4.9.B. at intervals from 11 p.m. until 2 a.m. with 7.7cm. Quiet day. No movement observed. Visibility poor.	B.
"	26.		Harassing fire carried out on NAVY TRENCH. Enemy shelled H.10 at intervals throughout the night by 7.7cm, H.18.a with 4.2" and H.6.c with 5.9". Parties seen in I.14.b.2.2. fired on & dispersed. Visibility poor.	B.
"	27.		S.O.S. shot carried out by 9/78 in 5 seconds. Harassing fire carried out on NAVY TRENCH, ROADS AND APPROACHES in accordance with 15th A.D.A. No.102. Hostile fire on H.9 from 9.6-11 p.m. FAMPOUX shelled with 5.9". Hostile batteries behind June R with good effect. Enemy aircraft active. Visibility fair.	B.
"	28		Brigade salvoes carried out from 7p.m to 8.30 p.m on WINDMILL COPSE, WHIP CROSS ROADS and SQUARE WOOD & during the night D. WASTE and MISK TRENCHES. Calibration carried out by Hos. Battery both forenoon & afternoon. Balloon Observation. Enemy shelled H & C and HQ with 4.1B.cm from direction of 1256. Visibility fair. Buring onslaught firing enemy sent up Red, golden-rain & yellow rockets from the front line. Yellow rocket appears to be SOS.	B.
"	29.		Rgll B.28/29th recd carried out on both sides of RAILWAY CUTTING I.14.b. with success.	B.

T2134. Wt. W708-776. 500000. 4/15. Sir J.C. & S.

WAR DIARY
INTELLIGENCE SUMMARY

July 1917, 78th Brigade R.F.A.

Place	Date	Hour	Summary of Events and Information	Remarks and references to Appendices
GAVRELLE – PLOUVAIN	29th (cont.)		Brigade fired a Barrage line in I.8.b and I.14.b and Lewis class in I.7 & I.9.a.O.O. No 103. Enemy shelled tracks – H.10.a. and at edit I.7. H.E. and Gas. Between 7p.m & 8 p.m one of our Nieuport planes flew very low over our front system of trenches & was heavy engaged by the enemy anti rifle & M.G. fire. Three times dived close to enemy first strong point blank range, finally dropping carefully.	R.1.
	30.		Enemy light Brigade arrived – WINDMILL COPSE, TRIANGLE APPROACHES, HORTLE fire moderate wide. Patrols of enemy in WHALE TRENCH fired on by Stand How. and dispersed.	
	31.		Brigade Salvoes carried out between 9 & 5 p.m & 12 & 4.5 a.m. on points of WART TRENCH and SHELLHOLES in I.8.d. Suspected TMB in I.2.c, I.2.a, J.2532 by Howitzers relieved. Enemy 15 c.m. Guns (H.V.) calibrated on POINT DU JOUR at 11.a.m & 11.45 a.m firing about 20 rounds. Enemy Trucks reviewed Stores – I.14.c and I.16.a, Fired on by Stand. How. and dispersed. Visibility for aerial activity below usual.	R.1.

AMMUNITION EXPENDED DURING JULY 1917

8056 A
4567 X
437 SK
5643 BX
506 BC BR
37 BTRR
27 BXT.

CASUALTIES:-

KILLED :- 1 Officer.
2. O. Ranks.

WOUNDED :- 4 O. Ranks.

WAR DIARY or INTELLIGENCE SUMMARY

Army Form C. 2118.

REF: TRENCH MAP: FRANCE 51B.N.W. 1:20,000.

AUGUST 1917. 78th BRIGADE, R.F.A.

Vol 26

Place	Date Augt	Hour	Summary of Events and Information	Remarks and references to Appendices
GAVRELLE	1.		Harassing fire carried out on NAVY TRENCH and I.3, 6 and d. Some shelling by enemy. Started firing along H.9 Harass. gun.	67.
PLOUVAIN	2.		Usual Harassing fire as per programme. Hostile Harass. nil. Enemy movement fired on and dispersed. Visibility fair.	B.
"	3.		Brigade observers at WINDMILL CORPS and WHIP CROSS ROADS. Hostile fire practically nil. Working parts in I.14, d.8.3 fired on and dispersed. Visibility poor.	B.
"	4.		Burst of fire on broken limber. Hostile fire practically nil. Parts of men seen in I.8.6, 6, 7, 9, and I.3.6. fired on and dispersed.	B.
"	5.		Burst of fire on trucks — I.8.d. carried out in accordance with 12 RFA. 00.111. A few enemy gas shells fell on front of Railway embkmt during the evening. Observation good. White Berry Lights fired from Mooch at C.28.d. 35, 80.	B.
"	6.		Barrage of shell fired in I.14, b+c and CANDY TRENCH in respect of ??? fly patrol in accordance with 60, 112 (P? R.S.A.). Hostile activity practically nil. Visibility poor.	B.
"	7.		Harassing fire on enemy howitzers. Hostile fire practically nil. Aerial activity, aerial torpedo parts reported at I.8, 8.14, b.5, I.8, b.50, fired on and dispersed. Visibility very poor.	B.

I

Army Form C. 2118.

WAR DIARY
or
INTELLIGENCE SUMMARY
(Erase heading not required.)

78th BRIGADE, R.F.A.

AUGUST 1917.

Place	Date	Hour	Summary of Events and Information	Remarks and references to Appendices
GAVRELLE - PLOUVAIN	8		Hostile fire opened at our forward area. At 3.45 a.m. SOS called sent up from the right of our front. Much heavy trench by enemy. The opened up above fired at 4.6 a.m. stopped at 4.35 a.m. & normal two guns gun.	
"	9		Very heavy hostile fire but normal hostile aircraft active.	B
"	10		Bombardment of SPROY TRENCH with Grenades and ANGELS TRENCH ago by howitzers. Retaliation open. A.M. 4.00. No 81. Hostile fire practically nil.	B
"	11		Quiet day. Hostile fire practically nil.	B
"	12		No round seen. SWALE TRENCH eng 3. SB D'Battery and SB D'Battery shared hits soared on apparently a "Very Light" and "Grenade store". Large volume of smoke ensured. Normal fire previously. Visibility good.	B
"	13		7.20 & 8.30 a.m. CREX TRENCH shelled intermittently with 5-9" 9.30 a.m. 6. 10.30 a.m. FAMPOUX-ATHIES Road shelled with 5-9". Enemy working about 10, 4.2. let P GAVRELLE ROAD in H9a. Visibility poor. Enemy fires on lock gate O15 & O16.	B
"	14		Quite fire D WIBBLE TRENCH from 3 to 57 a.m. & 11.50 p.m. opened up fire on LP. Fire in response & call from Infantry on our left "SOS RI" stopped 5 minutes later expected gas attack.	E

WAR DIARY
or
INTELLIGENCE SUMMARY.

Army Form C. 2118.

(Erase heading not required.) August 1917. 78th Brigade R.F.A.

Place	Date Aug.	Hour	Summary of Events and Information	Remarks and references to Appendices
GAVRELLE	15		Quiet effort on WIBBLE TR. and WINE GROSS ROAD. Bombardment of numerous WINE SHAFTS. Second French Mortars reported active. Quiet and silence by Hour Battery. Hostile artillery nil. Enemy party of about 50 men seen in MSK 7.8.21.04 fired on by "C" Battery and dispersed. Retaliation carried out. Bombardment of T.M. emplacements carried out by Hour Battery	D
"	16		in accordance with programme. Hostile gun practising nil. Hostile M.G. active.	D
"	17		Calibration carried out. Enemy aeroplane table Kench visitor active. Visibility very good.	D
"	18		Many enemy observation balloons up. Bombardment of Minks as stated in I.14.b, carried out as per O.O.3400.120. Enemy	D
"	19		Mortars reported active fired on and silenced by Hour Battery. Brig de relais at T.M. in I.2.c. At 9.45 a.m. several 5.9 fired at POINT DU JOUR otherwise all quiet and no enemy movement.	D
"	20		Harassing fire by 2 gun stacks as per O.O. 121. Between 10 a.m. and 10.30 a.m. enemy fired on WIBBLE during one outing by T.M.s. Enemy T.M.s reported active at WHIP ROAD POST. Fired on and silenced. Visibility fair.	D
"	21		Enemy T.M.s reported active fired on by Stokes and silenced. Hostile + 2cm culture POINT DU JOUR during morning. 10.5 a.m. Aust. friends #64. Book 4 flash below 0.23.C.20.20.	D

Army Form C. 2118.

WAR DIARY
or
INTELLIGENCE SUMMARY.

(Erase heading not required.)

August 1917. 78th Brigade, R.F.A.

Place	Date Aug.	Hour	Summary of Events and Information	Remarks and references to Appendices
GAVRELLE	22		Burst of fire 2 WACT, WAVY, WEED and SUIT TRENCHES and area beyond in accordance with O.O. 123. T.M's opened active fire & and silenced enemy movement & dispersed. Visibility fair.	A.
"	23		Bombardment of area between C37, T12 and WORK TRENCH and RAILWAY C37, & T12, 13, 7, 8. Carried out in order 13, 04, 94, 00, 124. Enemy fire NIL Our TRENCH dump on fire early & T17b. Hostile arty nil. Enemy movement & parties nil. Visibility good	B.
"	24		Bombardment with 4.5 How's. Gas Shell of RAILWAY CUTTING in I.3.d, 7.9, 6.7.9.c, 74 and B 18 Rhs. in accordance with No DKR 207/22. Bombardment WIETRENCH and areas behind B 18 Rhs in accordance 3 Sec. Battery. Visibility fair.	C.
"	25		T.M's opened active fire & and silenced. Enemy fire & various shapes in accordance with O.O. 125 (1 S.R.) T.M's opened active fire & and silenced. Visibility fair.	D.
"	26		Burst of fire & W.N.P CUTPERISON. Hostile bar raiding nil. Enemy movement in I.4.a.x & fired and dispersed. Hostile arty active. Visibility fair.	E.
"	27		Burst of fire in I.6.a and in accordance (2) 17 exed to T6, 127. Hostile T.M's & fired in accordance. Hostile preparations nil. Visibility fair.	F.
"	28		Hostile T.M's opened active fire & and silenced. Hostile fire on W.N.P's poor. Heavy rain during night.	G.

IV.

Army Form C. 2118.

WAR DIARY
or
INTELLIGENCE SUMMARY.
(Erase heading not required.)

AUGUST 1917. 70th Brigade R.F.A.

Place	Date	Hour	Summary of Events and Information	Remarks and references to Appendices
GAVRELLE - PLOUVAIN	29		Hostile T.M's reported active tris a bttns. Bakes and Telward. Otherwise hostile fire nil.	
	30		Enemy movement fired on and dispersed. Quiet day.	
	31		Bursts of fire at various objectives in accordance with 17th A.B.G. 12.B. Hostile fire nil. Visibility poor. Pistoe & enemy field artre dispersed. Calibration carried out. Hostile T.M's reported active tris R.a. Neighbourhood. Bursts of fire & various Beehives, South of Arras - Douai Railway in area marsh 17.40.7. 20.d.29. Burst of fire & suspected T.M. emplacement at junction of W17 and W.16.a.1. TRENCHES. Hostile fire practically nil. Aerial activity presents nil.	
			AMMUNITION EXPENDED :-	
			4532 A.	
			3427 AX.	
			23 ASK.	
			2731 Bx.	
			18 B.PS.	
			250 B9BR	
			67 BSK.	
			CASUALTIES :- NIL.	

V.

Army Form C. 2118.

WAR DIARY
or
INTELLIGENCE SUMMARY.

78th Brigade R.F.A.

SEPTEMBER 1917 Vol 27

Place	Date	Hour	Summary of Events and Information	Remarks and references to Appendices
GAVRELLE – PLOUVAIN	Sept. 1		Bursts of fire were carried out on Enemy roads and tracks. Hostile T.M.'s were silenced by 4.5 How. Signal bombing parties dispersed by 18 pdrs. Hostile fire practically nil. Visibility poor.	A.9.1
	2		A good deal bombardment of enemy dug-outs and trenches immediately preceded by 3 rounds gun fire with BX was carried out by 4.5 How. using lethal shells. 18 pdrs fired a working parties. Hostile fire was rather normal.	A.9.1
	3		Batteries calibrated. During the morning hostile T.M's were silenced. Enemy aircraft was active during early morning & evening. Visibility fair early but improved by evening. Quiet day.	A.9.1
	4		Calibration carried out by the battery observators. During the enemy Brigade area by 18 pdrs were fired on enemy working party. Bursts of fire from 10.30 pm to 11.15 pm were fired on enemy front line trenches & approaches in & about Divt. first. Hostile fire normal. FAMPOUX was shelled by 5.9 By during the afternoon and on Support lines shelled intermittently by 4.2 B.y. Hostile aircraft active. Visibility fair. A good deal of movement observed in back areas	A.9.1

Army Form C. 2118.

WAR DIARY
or
INTELLIGENCE SUMMARY.
(Erase heading not required.)

78th Bde. R.F.A.

September 1917

Place	Date	Hour	Summary of Events and Information	Remarks and references to Appendices
GAVRELLE – PLOUVAIN	Sept. 5		Harassing fire carried out and bursts of fire on tracks. T.M's silenced several times during early morning. Visibility bad. Quiet day.	W9R
	6		Hostile T.M's were active during early morning and were fired on by 18 pdrs. Between 5 – 5.30 p.m. a bombardment of enemy defences just N. of ARRAS – DOUAI RLY. Hostile artillery was more active than usual during the morning and carried out calibration on usual points. FAMPOUX was shelled intermittently. Aircraft active & many hostile balloons observed. Visibility good.	W9R
	7		Calibration carried out. At 6 p.m. a ten minute barrage on MART. TR. by 18 pdrs. was opened. At 9.45 p.m. the Brigade assisted the 62nd Div. ARTY. by covering with all 18 pdr. Btys. & Hvy. front line to 200x back and 4.5"s in Support Trenches for a Raid carried out by 62nd Div. which was successful. Hostile fire slow normal. Visibility bar.	W9R
	8		Early morning tar quiet. Hostile T.M's silenced by Brigade Orders at 11.30 am and 2.30 pm. At 6 pm – 6.30 pm all Batteries fired on a concentrated bombardment of enemy defences, dugouts & trenches near ARRAS – DOUAI RAILWAY. 18 pdrs. 500 rounds 4.5"s 150 rounds. At 10 p.m. the Brigade 18 pdrs. fired a	W9R

II

Army Form C. 2118.

WAR DIARY
or
INTELLIGENCE SUMMARY.
(Erase heading not required.)

Instructions regarding War Diaries and Intelligence Summaries are contained in F.S. Regs., Part II. and the Staff Manual respectively. Title pages will be prepared in manuscript.

Place	Date	Hour	Summary of Events and Information	Remarks and references to Appendices
Sept GAVRELLE - PLUVAIN	September 8 contd		"Lifting Barrage" fire a Raid by the Divl. Infantry to NIT & WOOD TRENCHES, & 5 Hrs Hombarded TRENCH JUNCTIONS and SUPPORT LINES. Hostile fire quiet during the day. In reply to Raid our support lines were shelled by TM's and 5.9's. Visibility poor.	A.W.D
	9		Usual Harassing fire carried out and working parties dispersed. Hostile fire quiet and visibility fair.	A.W.D
	10		Bursts of B. fire on enemy trenches at intervals during the night. 4.5 Hows. shelled T.M's. Hostile fire quiet. Visibility poor.	A.W.D
	11		Hostile TM's active during the day and several times silenced by L.S How. Occasional hostile Artillery fire on back areas. Trench & trench junctions kept under fire during the night.	A.W.D
	12		18 pdr. fired at intervals throughout the day and night on tracks carrying considerable enemy movement and probably Relays taking place. TM's again active. Visibility fair and enemy active.	A.W.D
	13		Day quiet. Usual harassing fire carried out. Visibility poor.	A.W.D
	14		Except for TM activity day quiet. Bursts of fire on tracks during the night	A.W.D

III

WAR DIARY or INTELLIGENCE SUMMARY

Army Form C. 2118.

Place	Date	Hour	Summary of Events and Information	Remarks and references to Appendices
GAVRELLE - PLOUVAIN	September 15		H.S.This consisted on T.M's in invention for forthcoming raid; 18/pdrs also carried at enemy fire. Day quiet and visibility poor.	W.D.
	16		At 9 p.m. all Batteries carried out fire for barrage and for a raid on Enemy Trenches by 51st Infantry Brigade. Raid successful and barrage reported excellent. Many dead Germans were found by raiding party on entering the Trenches. At 12 midnight (16th/17th) barrage and fire carried out for a raid by 52nd Infty. Bde. Raid very successful and Artillery fire reported very accurate. Many enemy killed also prisoners captured and two M/Guns. Hostile fire in reply to these raids was ragged and their barrage somewhat thin of the support lines received most attention. Visibility poor.	W.D.
	17		In retaliation for our successes on Trenches the previous day hostile Arty. showed considerable activity on our Trenches but very little damage was done. Btys. several times silenced hostile T.M's and opened fire. Salvos on Trenches opposite the heads of our line fired in by the enemy.	W.D.

IV

Army Form C. 2118.

WAR DIARY
or
INTELLIGENCE SUMMARY.
(Erase heading not required.)

Instructions regarding War Diaries and Intelligence Summaries are contained in F.S. Regs., Part II. and the Staff Manual respectively. Title pages will be prepared in manuscript.

Place	Date	Hour	Summary of Events and Information	Remarks and references to Appendices
GAVRELLE - PLOUVAIN	September 18		Bursts of fire during the night on tracks and trenches by 18 pdrs. and several harassing fire dispersed. Hostile fire on active than on the previous day.	W.D.
	19		Normal harassing fire carried out. Hostile fire below normal. Considerable activity by Enemy aircraft.	W.D.
	20		Day quiet. Occasional shelling of our support trenches during the day. Our Btys. dispersed working parties and fired on enemy movement.	W.D.
	21		Bursts of fire in accordance with Prog. opn. on tracks during the night. Hostile fire quiet. Aircraft again very active.	W.D.
	22		Normal harassing fire carried out. Day quiet and practically no hostile fire.	W.D.
	23		4.5 How. silenced T.M's during the night. 18 pdrs. carried out harassing fire. During the evening the Hostile fire below normal. Enemy aircraft active.	W.D.
			Enemy attempted to raid an trenches S.of Bke. 9m but was driven off A/78 fired at S.O.S. in response to S.O.S. During the enemy raid some attempt was also made to carry out neutralizing fire on our Batterys. One man slightly wounded but otherwise no damage done.	W.D.

V

Army Form C. 2118.

WAR DIARY
or
INTELLIGENCE SUMMARY.
(Erase heading not required.)

Instructions regarding War Diaries and Intelligence Summaries are contained in F.S. Regs., Part II. and the Staff Manual respectively. Title pages will be prepared in manuscript.

Place	Date	Hour	Summary of Events and Information	Remarks and references to Appendices
GAVRELLE- PLOUVAIN	September 24		Usual harassing fire and battery testing fired on. Hostile fire normal mostly by field guns.	W.I.P
"	25.		Day quiet. One section of each Battery was relieved by the opposite number of the 306th Bde in accordance with the relief of the 17th Div. by the 61st Division.	W.I.P
"	26.		Usual harassing fire. Hostile T.M's silenced by 4.5 How. Day quiet. Second section of each Battery relieved during the evening.	W.I.P
ST. NICHOLAS - ANZIN-W/Arras	27		Relief completed and B.H.Q. relieved by H.Q 306th Bde R.F.A. The Brigade remaining at their horse lines until relief of guns by T.O.M. is complete.	W.I.P / W.I.P
"	28		Brigade at horse lines.	W.I.P
"	29		" " " "	W.I.P
"	30		" " " " Supee'd B.G.C, R.A. Third Army.	W.I.P

Casualties
1 other rank wounded

Ammunition Expended
A 5711   AX 3687   BX 2654
BO9R 136 BSK 18   BXT 20

W.I.P Denott
2/Lt. R.F.a.
for O/C 78th Bde. R.F.A.

VI

WAR DIARY
INTELLIGENCE SUMMARY

Army Form C. 2118.

17bur 78th Bde. R.F.A.

OCTOBER 1917

Place	Date Oct.	Hour	Summary of Events and Information	Remarks and references to Appendices
			Reference maps BELGIUM Sheets 28 N.W., 20 S.W., 20 S.E. 1/20000	
ARRAS	1		The Brigade began entraining at 9.30am at ARRAS STATION	WD
HERZEELE BELGIUM	2		H.Q. arrived at GODWAERSVELDE at 9am followed by Batteries at intervals of 3-4 hrs and steamed immediately upon arrival, and from there proceeded by road to HERZEELE where the Bde was billeted for the night 2/3 Oct.	WD
Nr. ST. SIXTE	3		Orders were received at 12noon for the Bde. to proceed to new wagon lines at (A 8 0.2) Map Belgium Sht. 28 N.W.) near ST SIXTE and arrived there between 9pm + 11pm. The B'ty Commdrs. left HERZEELE earlier in the day to reconnoitre gun positions.	WD
LANGEMARCK	4		Advance parties and two guns per Bty. were ordered to go to gun positions Nr. 170 BOIS GITE (Map Ref. U 28 d MAP BELGIUM Sheet 20 S.W.) and ammunition was taken up during the night.	WD
"	5		Remaining guns taken into action and ammo taken up. Major C.M. CARROLL A/Lt. Lt. S. STRATTON 2/Lt. G.R. MOFFAT are wounded at gun positions during the morning. 7 O.R. killed + 7 O.R. wounded. Hostile fire action and positions shelled with 15cm.nvm. + 10 cm guns	WD
"	6		Batteries calibrated + HQ went out action. Hostile fire action and area shooting carried out. 2 O.R. wounded	WD
"	7		Calibration continued. Wagon Lines moved forward to ELVERDINGHE. 1 O.R. killed. 2 O.R. wounded ammunition taken up under heavy fire. I	WD

Army Form C. 2118.

WAR DIARY
or
INTELLIGENCE SUMMARY.
(Erase heading not required.)

Instructions regarding War Diaries and Intelligence Summaries are contained in F. S. Regs., Part II. and the Staff Manual respectively. Title pages will be prepared in manuscript.

Place	Date	Hour	Summary of Events and Information	Remarks and references to Appendices
LANGEMARCK	October 8		Calibration continued. Hostile fire active, 1 OR killed + 1 OR wounded whilst taking out and unloading ammunition.	A.9.D
"	9	5.25 am	Bde. took part in Operation N. of POELCAPPELLE - Barrage was placed immediately in front of Objective. Operation successful, guard placed towards objective taken. Hostile fire active. Capt. M.P. Glover B/78 wounded and 3 OR wounded early in the morning and O/C C/78 Major C.J.H. Marshall wounded through the thigh. Hostile counter attack repulsed. Bde O.P. established at WHITE TRR (U.23.d.9.1.)	A.9.D
"	10		Guns of previous day consolidated. Batteries registered new S.O.S lines (Capt. Belper Shot 20 SE Ref V.13.d 35.40 - V.13.d 55.85) Hostile fire active. 1 O.P. wounded. Barrage fired by all Btys. on S.O.S lines.	A.9.D
"	11		Continued shoot from 2.30 pm - 3 pm on STRING HOUSE (V.13.d) LANDING FM. and COMPROMIS FM. (V.13.b) strongly held by enemy. Forward O.P. established at "19 METRE HILL" (V.13.d 5.3) 3 OR wounded.	A.9.D
"	12		4th Div Arty Operation Order carried out, further ground gained N. of POELCAPPELLE. Hostile fire very active on our front lines and gun positions. Shell Shrapnel the day. 1 OR missing.	A.9.D

WAR DIARY
or
INTELLIGENCE SUMMARY.

(Erase heading not required.)

Army Form C. 2118.

Place	Date	Hour	Summary of Events and Information	Remarks and references to Appendices
LANGEMARCK	October 13		4th D.A. relieved by 34th D.A. under command of Brig. Gen. W. S. E. C. W. D. WALTHALL D.S.O. Command of Right Group. Right Artillery passed from Lt Col. A.G. ARBUTHNOT C.M.G. D.S.O. to Brig Gen. J.C. WRAY C.M.G. M.V.O. (57th D.A.). Personnel of B/78 proceeded to billets for 96 hrs rest. Hostile fire active. New S.O.S. line taken at (V.14.C.50.40 – V.14.a.75.25)	A/9/R
"	14		Day night harassing fire on areas beyond S.O.S. lines. E.A. very active and large numbers of GOTHAS bombed Bty positions H.B. and overrunt hangar lines. Hostile fire active on Bty positions attack area. 5 O.R. killed & 3 O.R. wounded	A/9/R
"	15		Hostile fire active AU BON GITE shelled constantly with 5.9" & 8". E.A very active and many bombing parties round back areas during the evening. 1 O.R. wounded.	A/9/R?
"	16		Calibration checked Hostile fire active on Bty positions. 1 O.R. killed and 3 O.R. wounded	A/9/R
"	17		At 8 am 17th D.A. transferred to Left Group of Right Artillery (evening 34th Div.) under command of Brig Gen. P. WHEATLEY D.S.O. New S.O.S. Line taken up (V.8.a.30.05 – V.8.a.30.45) H.S. Huo & DYCK F.M. & Huts. V.8.a 85.45. B/78 returned into action & A/78, D/78 returned to billets for 96 hrs rest. III	A/9/R

Army Form C. 2118.

WAR DIARY
or
INTELLIGENCE SUMMARY.
(Erase heading not required.)

Instructions regarding War Diaries and Intelligence Summaries are contained in F. S. Regs., Part II. and the Staff Manual respectively. Title pages will be prepared in manuscript.

Place	Date	Hour	Summary of Events and Information	Remarks and references to Appendices
LANGEMARCK	October 18		Reconnaissance carried out of Enemy front line, supports & hills behind, note barrage lines &c and report furnished to C.R.A. Bursts of fire on Enemy tracks of approach. Hostile fire active. E.A. active and very trying. Made talk by day & night. 1 O.R. killed. 3 O.R. wounded.	W.D.
	19		Calibration carried out. Hostile fire active and gun positions bombarded with gas shell. 3 O.R. gassed and sent to C.C.S. and many other slightly gassed. 5 O.R. wounded. A/75 & D/75 ordered to be in action by midnight.	W.D.
	20		Preliminary bombardment of 48 hrs commenced - on 18pdr firing 300 rds & 4.5 Hows. in 250 rds over the period. Hostile fire active & gun positions heavily shelled with 8", 5.9, 14.2, also a great many gas shells. 3 O.R. gassed & 3 O.R. wounded.	W.D.
	21		Bombardment continued. Batteries again heavily shelled. 9 O.R. wounded.	W.D.
	22		Operation Order commenced at 5.35 a.m. on Bpo Passchendaele front. 18pdr firing creeping barrage & 4.5 Hows. on strong points + fortified huts (V1 d 6.8). The weather was exceedingly bad and the mud rendered an advance almost impossible. Hostile fire active. 2nd Lt. J.S. Ranken 9/78 wounded, 2 O.R. wounded, 2 O.R. gassed. Batteries heavily shelled.	W.D.

IV

T2134. Wt. W708-776. 500000. 4/15. Sir J. C. & S.

WAR DIARY or INTELLIGENCE SUMMARY

Army Form C. 2118.

Place	Date	Hour	Summary of Events and Information	Remarks and references to Appendices
LANGEMARCK	Oct. 23		Hostile Arty & trench mortars active and positions shelled. Major W.H. Mackenzie 9/C/78 and 2/Lt. W.A. Cairns D/78 wounded. 1 OR wounded. Advance Bty positions reconnoitered at LANGEMARCK-POELCAPPELLE.	Ref. W.D. V.19 & V.24
"	24		Enemy eng'd him Bombardment prior to an attack. Our Bgps taking part. Hostile Artly active. 1 OR killed. 5 OR wounded. 2/Lt. S.H. Strand A/78 sent to hospital from effect of gas on the 19" & 20" inst.	W.D.
"	25		Preliminary bombardment continued Hostile fire active. 1 OR wounded. 1 OR gassed and 2 OR wounded by bombs in B/78 wagon lines. Hostile aircraft very active and many bombing raids.	W.D.
"	26		Our barrage at 5.40 am. for an attack. Then fired Creeping Barrage. H.S.A. mo fired on hostile huts (V.1.d) & concrete emplacements (V.2.c). The weather was again very bad and the mud prevented the contemplated advance. The Bgps were heavily shelled. Major L. Field, 2/Capt. P.S. Barker & Lt. Chantell R.O. of B/78 were killed by direct hit on burst shelter. 1 OR killed, 13 OR wounded. Several guns damaged & two destroyed.	W.D.
"	27		New S.O.S. lines registered V.8.a 0.6 & V.1.d 75.10. Bursts of fire on our usual SOS lines carried out. Hostile fire active. 6 Aircraft active and many bombing raids. 2 OR wounded (shell shock).	W.D.

WAR DIARY
or
INTELLIGENCE SUMMARY.
(Erase heading not required.)

Army Form C. 2118.

Place	Date	Hour	Summary of Events and Information	Remarks and references to Appendices
LANGEMARCK	October 28		Bursts of fire carried out in accordance with "Quiet" O.O. Hostile fire active. Bn. HQ's and Bty. positions shelled and gas shell in rear of Bty. Eyer in action Bttrs 10 & H.S.Mtrs 5. 2 O.R. wounded. E.A. very active and many bombing raids in vicinity of Bty. and Inf.y lines.	K.B.
"	29		Our fire consisted of "bursts" on tracks and roads. Hostile fire normal and a good deal of gas shell used round AU BON GITE, THE INNS and IRON CROSS ROADS and Bn. HQ at ADELPHI HOUSE. XIV Corps actived XII Corps. Sent harassing fire carried at active. 18cm Hz Bty. fired 200 rounds on V.23 Central and intermittent	19P
"	30		Shelling of AU BON GITE also with gas shell. E.A. active and many bombing raids. 1 O.R. wounded (gassed)	19P
"	31		Bursts of fire on our lines beyond S.O.S. line during the night. New S.O.S. lines taken up at 2pm (V.8.a.0.6 — V.1.d.8.3). Hostile shelling of STEENBEEK AREA throughout the day. Bn. HQ heavily shelled by 15cms + 10 cms from 4.45 pm — 5 pm. Hostile Aircraft exceptionally active and many bombing raids — bombs were dropped in PILCKEM VII	19P

WAR DIARY or INTELLIGENCE SUMMARY.

Army Form C. 2118.

Place	Date	Hour	Summary of Events and Information	Remarks and references to Appendices
LANGEMARCK	October 31	contd.	ROAD and a great many round wagon lines :-	N.D.

Summary

The month has been marked by the extremely bad weather, and its consequent mud, rendered taking of ammunition extremely difficult, and also the removal of damaged guns almost impossible. During the month 12 - 18 pdrs and 2 - 4.5 How were put out of action and had to be sent to I.O.M.; many minor casualties to guns were put right at Gun Position by Bty. fitters. The Gun Position were heavily shelled by En: 5.9 in, 4.2 & 7.7cm without ceasing for any length of time and the Bde. H.Q. were also heavily shelled at intervals, the roads & tracks leading to Batt were constantly fired on. Casualties were heavy, including in the 18th Bde. B.Gp., four Battery Commanders, one killed three wounded, two Capts. (2nd in Command) one killed, one wounded; Revd Lientt, one killed, five wounded. 18 OR killed 95 wounded Casualties to Horses amounted to about fifty.

VII

WAR DIARY
or
INTELLIGENCE SUMMARY

Place	Date	Hour	Summary of Events and Information	Remarks and references to Appendices
	October	Contd		
LANGEMARCK			Casualties. Officers Killed 3	
			" Wounded 9	
			Other Ranks Killed 18	
			" " Wounded 95	
			Total 125	
			Ammunition expended. A 18,698	
			AX 12,084	
			A Smoke 318	
			BX 8,093	
			B.S.K 933	
			B.C.B.R 990	

H.J. Dewot
Lt. R.F.A.
for O/Cmdg 78th Brigade R.F.A.

VIII

WAR DIARY
or
INTELLIGENCE SUMMARY

Vol 27
78th Bde. R.F.A.

NOVEMBER 1917

Place	Date	Hour	Summary of Events and Information	Remarks and references to Appendices
	November		Reference Map. BELGIUM Sheets 28 N.W. 20 S.W. 20 S.E. 1/20,000	
LANGEMARCK	1		Calibrations checked. Hostile fire quieter than usual. H.F. guns.	M.O.
"	2		Harassing fire carried out. Hostile fire on AU BON GITE, ADELPHI HSE and trench areas throughout the day. Enemy tk night gas shelling serious	M.O.
"	3		Bty positions. 2. O.R. gassed. Calibrations checked. Hostile fire active. G.o. bombardment of SCHREIBOOT AREA between 5 am + 5.55 pm Battery positions heavy shelled by 4.2" + 5.9" 3 O.R. gassed.	M.O.
"	4		Bursts of fire carried out on Tonkin Trench. Enemy fire rather normal. Intermittent fire round Battery positions. 1 O.R. wounded. 12 gassed.	M.O.
"	5		Harassing fire by enemy Artillery on AU BON GITE. E. aircraft active. And many bombing raids on our second bayon Line 3 O.R. wounded. 1 O.R. missing 1917	M.O. 1917
"	6		Bombardment by all Batteries on area beyond our S.O.S. Lines from 6am – 6.45am. Enemy heavy shelled LANGEMARCK, AU BON GITE and STEENBEEK. Visibility low. E. aircraft active + bombing parties during the evening. 3 O.R. killed. 3 O.R. wounded. 5 gassed.	M.O.
"	7		Batteries prepared ready to track from to be covered in the 8th inst. Enemy	1

WAR DIARY
or
INTELLIGENCE SUMMARY.
(Erase heading not required.)

Army Form C. 2118.

Place	Date	Hour	Summary of Events and Information	Remarks and references to Appendices
	November			
LANGEMARCK	7th	Only	Line taken normal 3 M.R. guard	N.D.
	8		All 18 pdr. Btys. withdrew their guns and proceeded to Bryn Lewis. H.Q./Bns. moved 2 Hrs.	N.D.
ELVERDINGHE	9		Brigade remained at Bryn Lewis. Remaining Hrs. removed from position	N.D.
PROVEN.	10		The Brigade left for PROVEN where they were billeted for the night	N.D.
NOORDPEENE	11		The Brigade marched to NOORDPEENE and Bths. at billets there	N.D.
"	12		The Brigade in rest at NOORDPEENE.	N.D.
"	13		"	N.D.
"	14		Training commenced	N.D.
"	15		Training of Btys. carried out	N.D.
"	16		"	N.D.
"	17		"	N.D.
"	18		"	N.D.
"	19		"	N.D.
"	20		"	N.D.
"	21		"	N.D.

Army Form C. 2118.

WAR DIARY
or
INTELLIGENCE SUMMARY.
(Erase heading not required.)

Instructions regarding War Diaries and Intelligence Summaries are contained in F. S. Regs., Part II. and the Staff Manual respectively. Title pages will be prepared in manuscript.

Place	Date	Hour	Summary of Events and Information	Remarks and references to Appendices
	November			
NOARDPEENE	22		Brigade in Rest and training Carried out	A.R
"	23		"	A.R
"	24		"	A.R
"	25		"	A.R
"	26		"	A.R
"	27		"	A.R
"	28		"	A.R
"	29		"	A.R
"	30		"	
			Casualties. 3 O.R. killed	
			4 O.R. wounded	
			32 O.R. gassed	
			1 O.R. missing	
			Ammunition Expended. A 1031	
			AX 197	
			BX 817	

W.J. Dever / Lt. R.F.A.
Ar.O/C. 78th Bty. R.F.A.

Army Form C. 2118.

WAR DIARY
or
INTELLIGENCE SUMMARY.
(Erase heading not required.)

78th Brigade R.F.A.
DECEMBER 1917.

WM 30

Place	Date 1917	Hour	Summary of Events and Information	Remarks and references to Appendices
NOORDPEENE	Decr 1		The Brigade in rest at NOORDPEENE (near CASSEL). Training of Batteries carried on daily.	
"	2		"	
"	3		"	
"	4 & 5		"	
"	15		"	
"	16		The Brigade marched to ECQUES en route for 3rd Army Area.	
"	17		" " " Bours MARST	
"	18		" rested at "	
"	19		" marched to REBRIEVIETTE	
"	20		" " " "	
"	21		" marched to HAUTEVILLE	
"	22		" rested at "	
"	23		" rested at "	
"	24		" marched to Q [?] le COUPE (Arrivederci [?])	
"	25		" " " Le TRANSLOY	
"	26		" " took over at ETRICOURT	

WAR DIARY or INTELLIGENCE SUMMARY

Army Form C. 2118.

Place: RIBECOURT
78th Brigade, R.F.A.
1917

REF. MAP. MARCOING:- 57 C, NE 4. 1:10,000.

FRANCE: 57 C. 1: 40,000.

Date	Hour	Summary of Events and Information	Remarks and references to Appendices
DEC. 26.		Our sector per Battery and sector pertaining to 2nd Brigade R.F.A. (6 Howitzers) in rear and and out of RIBECOURT. Guns later are in position.	R.2.
27		Relief of remainder of Batteries completed 12 noon when command of his Field Artillery Group (consisting of 78 Bde. B/155 A.F.A. and B/155 A.F.A.) 19th Aus. Artillery passed to 2.1.S.C. R. Shangenberg 3rd Command 75th Bde, A/155, B/155 Group Headquarters L.31d central (HINDENBURG LINE) Battery positions in Q.6, a, + c and 18 Pdr. Anti-tank gun forward L.21d.com. 9 p.m. to 12·15 a.m Bursts of fire in L.22, Q,6, L.6. L22 c, 40, 45.	R.2.
28.		Sunny morning – enemy shelled sunken paths of RIBECOURT until 4.20 army the night. Reconnaissance carried out showing that enemy headquarters at C of 2 Dr Sauer J.21.72 ascendancy unused miles. Night on guns yesterday - night in rear. Observation-shelling of Ribecourt. Snipers on new trench of enemy unsupported and discovered. Pte 18 Pdr. take fire After dawn to purpose of support forward base to Battery positions before dark. Parties for patrolls till.	R.2.
29.	6.30 a.m	Enemy heavily bombarded 63rd Divisional front in our right + made a raid succeeding in small parties of our trench. Bombardment eased till about 8.30 a.m. during which time our Battery positions were heavily shelled with gas shells (alleged). No casualties, 2/75.	R.2.

Army Form C. 2118.

WAR DIARY
or
INTELLIGENCE SUMMARY.

(Erase heading not required.)

78th Brigade, R.F.A.

DECEMBER 1917.

Place	Date	Hour	Summary of Events and Information	Remarks and references to Appendices
RIBECOURT	Dec. 1-30(cont)		and 12 O.R. wounded (B.O.R.) + 6 O.R. gassed (gas poisoning). Enemy holds front trench Ribecourt opposite D.508. This is at present defended ; Capts. Parry Coll. came around A/78, D/78. Enemy again bombarded & raided Boisieres trench in our (of 5th, but without success along part of the front. I gained position. At request of Infantry opened up fire on S.O.S. line Ribecourt (5.15 am to 6 am) during the bombardment. 1 O.R. wounded 11R (gunner) 78.	B.F.
	31	4 am to 7 am. Battery position shelled 77 mm gas shell (phosgene) about 300 rounds.	
			Casualties :- 1 Officer (Major A.E. Nelson MC) wounded. Ammunition expended :-	A 1121.
			1 Officer (2 Lt Boulter) accidentally wounded.	AX 1539.
			13 O.R. wounded (O.W.)	BX 951.
			6 O.R. gassed	
			Honours awarded :- A/Major A.E. Haynes A/78 - Bar to Military Cross	
			A/Major A.E. Wright A/78 :- Military Cross.	
			A/Major L. Field (Killed) B/78 } Mentioned in	
			A/Major O.F.K. Marshall D/78 } Despatches.	
			A/Major R.A.E. Wright B/78 &	
			A/Captain W.F. Parrington C/78 }	

R.T.W., Lt Col
1 I/c 78 (?)

WAR DIARY
or
INTELLIGENCE SUMMARY. 78th BRIGADE, R.F.A.

Army Form C. 2118.

JANUARY 1918. REF. MAP. FRANCE. SHEET 57C. VOL 31

Place	Date 1918	Hour	Summary of Events and Information	Remarks and references to Appendices
RIBECOURT	1	8pm - 6am (2)	Bursts of fire on SUNKEN ROAD in L16d and 17c. 12 minutes to 2a.m. Enemy shelled 'Belly' behind Battery positions in Q.6a, a.& c with 5.9, 4.2 and 77 M.M gas shell – about 500 rounds.	D.
	2		One section per Battery of 19th D.A. relieved one section per Battery of 78th Bde. Relieved section with drew to Wagon lines at RUYAULCOURT. Showing fire commenced.	D.
	3		Remainder of Bde. relieved by 19th D.A. (87th Bde.). The battery personnel of the Bde. relieved one section per Battery of 2nd D.A. (35th Bde.) near the cutt-out S. HERMIES. (K.26 & K.32).	D.
	4		Remainder of Bde. took over from 283.A. and 17th D.A. Organised anew group under command of Lt. Col. K.R. George KIRKE DSO Brigade began here & received at RUYAULCOURT. Battery positions in K.26.c; K.32.a; H.R. 7.b; 6; 8; 17. K.26, c, D, 7; 1; 7. Relief of 2nd Divisional Infantry by B 17th Divisional Infantry completed.	D.
			S.O.S. lines taken up K.11, a, 00, 80 - K.4, c, 65, 45 - K.3d, 05, 45. Artillery covering 17th Division consists of 235th & 236th Bdes. (47 D.A.) 17th D.A.S. & 93 A.F.A. Bde.	
	5/6		Guns calibrated and harassing fire carried out.	D.

Army Form C. 2118.

WAR DIARY
or
INTELLIGENCE SUMMARY.
(Erase heading not required.)

JANUARY 1918 78th Brigade RFA

Place	Date	Hour	Summary of Events and Information	Remarks and references to Appendices
HERMES - HAVRINCOURT	January 7.		Hostile shelling of HAVRINCOURT, FLESQUIÈRES and HERMIES normal. Usual harassing fire carried out.	A.
	8.		236 & 238 Btys RGA Ranged on to 47 HOWR. New OPs being taken up by the Bde. K12.c, 10.00 - K11.a, 0.0 - K10.a, 9.0, 8.5. Harassing fire on pontoons/tracks leading to GRAINCOURT carried out.	A.
	9.		Took a few points of C/78 (K.31, c, 2, 4) carried BR. Hostile shelling of HAVRINCOURT cloth. Usual harassing fire on pontoon tracks and approaches carried out by our Artillery.	A.
	10.		Hostile battery park in camouflage numbers reported on the BAPAUME - CAMBRAI ROAD in E.28 & E.29 & CUILATIN carried out. Hostile fire practically nil. Aerial activity on both above normal. 8.30 p.m. to 8.40 p.m. "Gasbose" flares	A.
	11.		Guns on roads trenches and approaches. Shot many flatulite R protruded. 5.30 a.m. Bn. Shoots in K11 a b & K c b Harassing fire carried out during night. Hostile fire cnth.	A.

Army Form C. 2118.

WAR DIARY
or
INTELLIGENCE SUMMARY.

(Erase heading not required.) 78th BRIGADE R.F.A.

JANUARY 1918

Instructions regarding War Diaries and Intelligence Summaries are contained in F. S. Regs., Part II. and the Staff Manual respectively. Title pages will be prepared in manuscript.

Place	Date	Hour	Summary of Events and Information	Remarks and references to Appendices
HARNES	JANUARY 12.		Calibration carried out. Reconnaissance carried out 4.20 and 5.30 throughout the day from direction of BURLON WOOD. Hostile planes flew over our lines and battery positions. Harassing fire carried out by our artillery.	A.
	13.		Registration of Runs No. 2 at T.3.b. 6.7.4. (next to Right Section Infantry Brigade). Hostile fire slight. Harassing fire carried out.	A.
	14.		Burst of fire on SUNKEN ROAD in K.6.C. Hostile fire and harassing fire and movement practically nil. Visibility poor.	A.
	15.		Harassing fire - hostile fire slight.	A.
	16.		6.50 p.m. to 7.50 p.m. Bursts of fire every few minutes & harassing fire on K.4.b.d. and K.5.c. in view of expected enemy relief.	A.
	17.		Sept. Bursts of fire on HAWKIN COURT, HERNIER and FONTAINE at 5, 4, 20, 5.40 and 7.7 and a.m. Usual harassing fire on enemy tracks trails & approaches carried out by our artillery. 18 Battery moves to position in K.31.e.3t.	A.
	18.		Hostile battery active at E.22.d.20.90 engages Boxmahling trenches. Battery positions checked. Will 4.2 pm & 5-7 Hrs. 18 O.R. Howitzers, Battery positions heavily shelled with 4.2 pm to 5-7 Hrs. 18 O.R. Howitzers fire hostile planes flew over our lines in direction of HAVRINCOURT. Hostile plane engaged	A.
	20.			A.

Army Form C. 2118.

WAR DIARY
or
INTELLIGENCE SUMMARY. 78th BRIGADE, R.F.A.

(Erase heading not required.)

JANUARY 1916.

Place	Date	Hour	Summary of Events and Information	Remarks and references to Appendices
HERMIES	January 20.		by our planes and marked clouds in enemy lines. No 2 Lyr Lines to Rupaucourt 6 VELU (P25Q).	B.
"	21.		Registration carried out. Hermies shelled by enemy during the day from direction of BOURLON WOOD. Visibility poor. Usual harassing fire carried out.	B.
"	22.			
"	23.		Usual harassing fire carried out. Hostile fire slight. Ho[stile] Contact aeroplane hrs.	B.
"	24.			
"	25.		Registration carried out. Hostile fire active, hostile planes active, liven barrage at 5.20 ALBATROSS oversawn liver fired at by AA a short while off. Visibility fair.	B.
"	26.		Visibility very bad - Kite fog. Hostile fire, movement aeroplane activity NIL. Usual fire and troop approaches in train on wet.	B.
"	27.			
"	28.		Further patrol in E.28.b. found 32 by our Artillery and dispersed. Hostile fire slackens all morning. our artillery & found trenches. Registration carried out. Hostile movement in E.23.Q.9.0, were dispersed.	B.
"	29.		Visibility fair. Bursts of fire & enemy ports & trenches by our artillery. Hostile Contact plane flew over T36 & dropped 4 at our various of Trench areas.	B.

WAR DIARY or INTELLIGENCE SUMMARY

78th Brigade R.F.A.

January 1916

Place	Date	Hour	Summary of Events and Information	Remarks and references to Appendices
HERNIES	30.		Hostile shelling of front line, HAVRINCOURT and HERMIES till 4.20 and 5.90. Reprisals carried out. Harassing fire 12 rounds trench expenditure. Hostile planes active. Enemy bombing planes passed over Battery positions & dropped many bombs in rear area, during afternoon hostile balloon put in flames.	B2
	31.		Intermittent hostile shelling & sniping of our positions. Enemy fire M.G. shrill harassing fire carried out on our Artillery. During the month a great deal of plane and balloon expended on positions in our supply and Communication (9/12) new M.Gs and new hinges twice. Rear positions also permitted in connexion with 17th Divisional Defence Scheme.	B2
			Casualties :- 1 O.R. wounded. 1 O.R. killed.	P7.
			Ammunition Expended: A 2604. A 2707. B 1740. 8 GR. 135.	
			NEW YEARS HONOURS LIST :- M/Major L. FIELD M.C. (Adjutant) awarded the D.S.O. 2/Lt J. SIMPSON R.H. 2/Major C.F.R. MARSHALL 5th awarded the D.S.O. (signed)	

WAR DIARY or INTELLIGENCE SUMMARY

Army Form C. 2118.

Vol 32

78th Brigade R.F.A.

FEBRUARY 1918. MAP: FRANCE. SHEET 57c. Ed.2. 1:40,000.

Place	Date	Hour	Summary of Events and Information	Remarks and references to Appendices
HERMIES	1918 Feb. 1		Hostile shelling of HAVRINCOURT and HERMIES at 2.20 and 5.70. Retaliation carried out. Harassing fire on roads & tracks out approaches from GOUZEAUCOURT.	R.
	2		Personal 4.2 rounds 2 HAVRINCOURT and K22 6 during day. 10.45 a.m. 2nd Lt. B.F.W. AVIATIK Observer engaged by S.E.5 and forced with a crash on our lines near SPOIL HEAP in T36a.	F.
	3		Retaliation carried out. Intermittent harassing fire on tracks and approaches. Lieut. Nutt hostile shelling of HERMIES, HAVRINCOURT and valley positions in K26c.	R.
	4		Harassing fire carried out on roads and approaches to HERMIES. Burst fire schedule — K8c and d and 5 rounds went to trenches and enemy trenches. 77b and 77c instructive, Scale 77, Demiladen bombing 26/2. 77.30 in K14 and open 17"XR instructive, Scale 77 Demiladen bombing 26/2. 73a in K10b followed by an enemy unsuccessful pull in one of our trenches.	R.
	5		Usual harassing fire carried out. Lieutenant Rutledge J. Harrison and HAVRINCOURT at 6.75 am 21.20 5.50am. Stars 77 Bombardment and Bulleris gun fire on S.O.S. lines violet pale white shelling ceased at 7 am.	F.
	6		Retaliation carried out. Portzan hostile & dispersal. Occasional ammunition or HERMIES, HAVRINCOURT near H Sprint and on back areas.	R.

Army Form C. 2118.

WAR DIARY
or
INTELLIGENCE SUMMARY.

78th Brigade RFA (Erase heading not required.) FEBRUARY 1918.

Instructions regarding War Diaries and Intelligence Summaries are contained in F. S. Regs., Part II. and the Staff Manual respectively. Title pages will be prepared in manuscript.

Place	Date 1918	Hour	Summary of Events and Information	Remarks and references to Appendices
HERMIES	Feb. 7.		Hostile part at E26.b fired on and dispersed. Hostile fire - 5-50 on Hermies and Havrincourt intermittently during the day.	B.
"	" 8.		Usual harrassing fire and registration carried out. Hostile fire. Aerial activity at movement nil.	B.
"	" 9.		Registration carried out. Burst of fire on Hermies and Fermicourt and trenches in K4.b. Hostile fire probably Mt. Carrie activity no Red.	B.
"	" 10.		Harrassing fire carried on roads, tracks and approaches. Hermies and Havrincourt shelled 4.20 and 5.50 intermittently throughout the day. Movement of small parties generally in E 28 & fired on and dispersed. Visibility fair, aerial activity normal.	B.

Army Form C. 2118.

WAR DIARY
or
INTELLIGENCE SUMMARY.
(Erase heading not required.)

FEBRUARY 1918   78th BRIGADE R.F.A.

Place	Date 1918	Hour	Summary of Events and Information	Remarks and references to Appendices
HERMIES	Feb 11th		Mur 4.5 Hows carried out shoot on E.28.a and J.22.b using visual signalling. Battery positions shelled by hostile 4.12 and 5 inch apparently from captive balloon. Aerial activity slight.	B.T.
"	" 12		Harrass and Battery parties in E.28.a and J.30 engaged by over 15 Pairs Aerial activity nil, visibility bad. Visual harassing fire carried out.	B.T.
"	" 13		Burst of fire on Honda and TRAELS and CATTRENCH in K.4.d. Very little movement seen, aerial activity nil and visibility very bad.	B.T.
"	" 14		Hostile T.M. active in K.3.c and K.4.d at fine 22 and released. Bursts of fire on GRAINCOURT. Harrass'ment N12. Lots visibility.	B.T.
"	" 15		Battery parties in K.3.a fired on and dispersed. Bursts of fire on GRAINCOURT and harassing fire. Hostile bombing plane (GOTHA) completed through night trouble to land in our lines in P.21 – the crew consisting of one officer and 3 O.R.'s captured.	B.T.
"	" 16		Bursts of fire from 7pm to 10pm on trenches and harras'ment roads of approach. Enemy relief. Battery positions shelled by hostile 5.9 and 7.7 gas shell. Hostile aircraft active.	B.T.

Army Form C. 2118.

WAR DIARY
or
INTELLIGENCE SUMMARY.
(Erase heading not required.)

78th BRIGADE, RFA.

February 1918.

Place	Date 1918	Hour	Summary of Events and Information	Remarks and references to Appendices
HERMIES	Feb.17.		Hostile T.Ms engaged by Hos. 3 Battery and silenced. Harassing fire during night on new Y.M. roads at Heudicourt, HAVRINCOURT and interference with Battn F.9.0. Hostile planes active, Bigson containing propaganda dropped on our lines from hostile plane. Sub Flights active intermittently.	R.T.
"	" 18.		Large working parties in ABear.L engaged and dispersed. Usual harassing fire. Hostile Battery S.H.HAVRINCOURT in particular & no. 79 spasmodic.	R.T.
"	" 19.		4.5 How. observed GRAINCOURT with gas shell in reply to hostile shelling Gouzeaucourt line and HAVRINCOURT with Gas shell. Aerial activity above normal.	R.T.
"	" 20.		Usual harassing fire. Hostile fire above normal. S.9 shells Battery positions. It was apparently harassing on movie bridge near 176. Y.13. Seems heavy fearing taken to flanks.	R.T.
"	" 21.		Hostile movement seen and engaged. Usual harassing fire in main road and approaches. Ridge for Trescault not during the day. Heavy T.M. fire on our trenches about LA and a fast burst of Geek shells on neighbourhood of Battery positions.	R.T.

Army Form C. 2118.

WAR DIARY
or
INTELLIGENCE SUMMARY.
(Erase heading not required.)

Instructions regarding War Diaries and Intelligence Summaries are contained in F.S. Regs., Part II. and the Staff Manual respectively. Title pages will be prepared in manuscript.

Place: 78th BRIGADE R.F.A.
FEBRUARY 1918.

Place	Date 1918	Hour	Summary of Events and Information	Remarks and references to Appendices
HERMIES	Feb 22.		Usual posts & ranging fire & & dispersed. Hostile fire practised nil during the day. Enemy's T.M.s also nil. A below positive as per enemy. Aerial activity practically nil.	A.
"	" 23.		Usual harassing fire & roads & approaches - Bombarded J.7.7.0 in line with Naval Reserve Wy MACKENZIE Having petitioned for England to petels command 5/78. and at 3.15 a.m. an infantry patrol under Puppy Trench occupied Hostile fire above normal. RAVENCOURT WOOD in K.27d. and K.32b. his forces for B.6.O considered Hoplite Kenny. Hostile night firing on our artillery.	B.
"	" 24.		Nightfiring carried on as normal. At night hostile fire above normal on HAPLINCOURT and FLESQUIERES. Aerial activity practically nil.	C.
"	25.			D.
"	26.		Normal night firing. Hostile working parties engaged & dispersed. Hostile shelling of HERMIES at 8.20 a.m. by 15 cm. H.V. HV. Hostile aerial activity above normal. Kite balloon.	E.
"	27.		Registration carried out. N.F. also taken up by howrs during the day. HAPLINCOURT shelled intermittently throughout the day by 5.9" and 7.7.	F.

Army Form C. 2118.

WAR DIARY
or
INTELLIGENCE SUMMARY.

(Erase heading not required.)

78 Brigade R.F.A. FEBRUARY 1918.

Place	Date 1918	Hour	Summary of Events and Information	Remarks and references to Appendices
HERNIES	Feb 28		Registration carried out. 11.50 a.m. to 1 p.m. 8 in. and 5.5 Hows batteries established O.Ps. in K.22.b. with aeroplane observation. Later the aeroplane engaged ground targets in K.22.b. with machine gun fire. Throughout the month the batteries have worked hard on keeping in positions, reserve positions for various lines of defence and positions for reinforcing Brigade are well ahead in the forward lines at V.7.L.W. Casualties :- 3 O.R. wounded (A/78) 1 officer died in hospital. Ammunition Expended :- A. 2066; A.X. 3609; B.X. 341; BdBR. 300. Honours and Awards :- No. 92709 Secgt. A. ARCHBALD (C/78). No. 70107 Bdr. W. EASTEN (A/78). } BELGIAN CROIX de GUERRE. New Years Honours List :- Sergt F.J. SQUIRE (A/78) No. 10275 Gnr F.T. AUGER (A/78) M.S.M.	

R. Tolkitt
Capt R.A. for R.
for O.C. 78—

17th Div.

Headquarters,

78th BRIGADE, R.F.A.

M A R C H

1 9 1 8

WAR DIARY
or
INTELLIGENCE SUMMARY.

(Erase heading not required.)

78th Brigade R.F.A.

7th March 1918.

Place	Date	Hour	Summary of Events and Information	Remarks and references to Appendices
HERMIES	1918 March 7		Shot 57 & E2 2 L40.07 R.J. Maj. Irwine	
	1		Registered and obtained on GRAIN COURT with R.J further FLESQUIERES and HARINCOURT shelled slightly.	m.O
	2		Usual harassing fire carried out on hostile engineers.	m.O
	3		Registration cannot obs. stable for present. N.R.	m.O
	4		Worked party at E26.b fired on & dispersed – Visibility poor.	m.O
	5		Registration carried out. Some shelling of HERMIES.	m.O
	6		Parados of trench at shot Irwine, tracks seen from visibility enemy.	m.O
	7		4.5 How shelled GRAIN COURT with R.J. for details enemy shelling below normal. Visibility low.	m.O
	8		Usual harassing fire. Hostile fire above normal. Battery positions shelled by 5.9 S.H.E front Visibility low enquiry down to angle.	m.O
	9		Enemy new work pads. Jam. Hostile artillery below normal.	m.O
	10		Small parties of enemy fired on & dispersed. Hostile fire below N.R. Visibility fair.	m.O

WAR DIARY
or
INTELLIGENCE SUMMARY

Army Form C. 2118.

MARCH 1918. Sheet 57C. S.E. 1/40,000
76.D.2.6.6.B.

Place	Date	Hour	Summary of Events and Information	Remarks and references to Appendices
HERMIES	11.		Reg. Maj. FRANKS. Registration carried out. HAYRENCOURT SIDING during the day. Visibility poor	m.
	12		About harassing fire carried out on roads, approaches Bombardment of 7 T.M.s in K.46.c.d at 3.15 p.m.—	m.
	13.		Lays & working parties on BITTEN road engaged — Registration carried out —	m.
	14		Hostile movement in GRAINCOURT area engaged. Hostile planes active	m.
	15.		Registration carried out. Visibility low.	m.
	16.		Registration carried out — HAYRINCOURT — HAYRINCOURT SIDING shelled during the day.	m.
			Harassing fire carried out on roads, tracks & HERMIES & HAYRINCOURT shelled by 4.2 & 5.9	m.
	17.		Hostile harass. fire registration carried out.	m.
	18		Occasional shelling of HAYRENCOURT during the day. Visibility low.	m.

WAR DIARY or INTELLIGENCE SUMMARY

Army Form C. 2118.

(Erase heading not required.) 76th Brigade R.F.A.

Ref: MAP FRANCE Sheet 57c Ed 2 1:40,000

Place	Date	Hour	Summary of Events and Information	Remarks and references to Appendices
HERMIES	Mch.19		Harrassing fire carried out. Enemy activity normal. Visibility poor.	mO
	20.		HAVRINCOURT & HERMIES shelled by 4.2 & 5.9 — Harrassing fire on GRAINCOURT & Havrincourt.	mO
	21.		A & D Batteries lightly shelled about 5 am with H.E. Gas & H.E. shells were continued intermittently throughout the day. Enemy preparation started 5 am & lifted 5:30. Our infantry were attacked in force about 9 am & were forced to leave HUGHES trench. All batteries continued on S.O.S. lines throughout the day. Some 700 rounds per gun fired by the Brigade. Orders were received at 11pm to retire to reserve position on J.35.c. This retirement was carried out by 3.0 am. A Battery destroyed their anti tank gun before leaving #D770. Closing up their forward hours.	mO

Army Form C. 2118.

WAR DIARY
or
INTELLIGENCE SUMMARY.
(Erase heading not required.)

78th Brigade R.H.A.

March 1918. France.

Ref. Map. France Sheet 57c. C.a.2. 1/40,000

Place	Date	Hour	Summary of Events and Information	Remarks and references to Appendices
	1918 March 22.		All Batteries in action 7.35.a.m. and all firing steadily on front front between HERMIES and HAVRINCOURT. Heavy enemy attacks took place throughout the day but were held up by our infantry. Batteries attacked during the afternoon by hostile aeroplanes with machine guns.	W.O.
	23rd		Orders to retire were received about 9.0 a.m. when "B" & "D" Batteries took up a position just South of BERTINCOURT & 6 guns of "B" rear guard action. "A" & "C" retired 1-30 p.m. passing through "B" & "D" who then followed, the whole Brigade assembled at ROCQUIGNY. Moving again the Brigade bivouaced at BEAULANCOURT.	W.O.
	24		Orders were received 5.0 a.m. for batteries to come into action and cover retirement of 2nd Divn through the 17th. This was done "B" and "D" Batteries taking up forward and "A" and "C" in rear. Midway the whole line was ordered to retire 6/18 being left as rearguard. The next place of assembly was between LE SARS and MARTINPUICH. The Batteries coming into action line but not firing. The night was spent at POZIERES.	W.O.
	25"		5.0 a.m. orders were received for Brigade to come into action by batteries in action by 8.10 a.m. to cover a line in front of DELVILLE WOOD. This was done and batteries in action by 8.10 a.m. At 12 noon signs of enemy movement were seen in MAMETZ and BAZENTIN-LE-PETIT WOODS. One gun A/78 and one gun C/78 came down were run forward on to the crest and starting at a range of 1200 came down to 650 yds, firing through telescopic sights at the advancing enemy. 800 R⁰ were fired by these guns which completed smashed up the enemy attack. Ammunition then exhausted the guns were withdrawn and Batteries ret'd again W.O. at BECOURT from where they were ordered to BOUZENCOURT where they spent the night.	W.O.

D. D. & L., London, E.C. (A7001) Wt. W2771/M2931 750000 5/17 Sch. 51 Forms C.2. o/14

Army Form C. 2118.

WAR DIARY
or
INTELLIGENCE SUMMARY.
(Erase heading not required.)

Ref: Maps France ALBERT. Combined Sheet { 57D S.E., 57C. S.W., 62D. N.E., 62C. N.W. }

Place	Date	Hour	Summary of Events and Information	Remarks and references to Appendices
	26.		Batteries came into action around SENLIS "B" battery being forward and remained in reserve enemy attacks held up all along line	MTP
	27.		A178 took section forward into open but were unfortunately observed by the enemy and had both guns put out of action.	MT
	28.		Harassing fire carried out during day and night on approaches to	MO
	29. 30.		ALBERT. SENLIS slightly shelled by H.E. during the morning. Registration was carried out - Visibility good. Harassing fire carried out during the day and night - Aerial activity on a slight increase. 2 of E.A. driven back by our Anti-Aircraft Guns.	MO MO
	31.		MILLENCOURT shelled intermittently by H.E. during the afternoon - Visibility low.	MO

Ammunition Expended. Approx.   A 60,000   Ax 30,000   Bx 25,000

Casualties :- 3 Officers Wounded.
3. O.R. Killed.
25. O.R. Wounded.

[signature]
Capt. 7.Bgl.
For O.C. 7 Bde 9.7A

17th Divisional Artillery

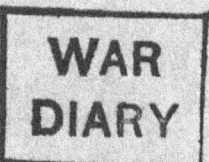

78th BRIGADE R. F. A.

APRIL 1918

WAR DIARY or INTELLIGENCE SUMMARY

(Erase heading not required.)

76th Brigade R.F.A. Army Form C. 2118.

April 1918

Place	Date	Hour	Summary of Events and Information	Remarks and references to Appendices
SENLIS	1918 April 1		Calibration carried out. Harassing fire on approach. Movement engaged on PRICOURT ROAD. Normal activity slight.	AA
	2		Registration carried out. Normal harassing fire meant penetration. EAST of ALBERT. Visibility poor.	AA
	3		Registration carried out. Normal harassing fire. EA rather more active.	AA
	4		Normal harassing fire on approach and junctions - TMs in W27N engaged by them with good results. At 12pm enemy put down very hostile TM bombardment on front line, later reported attacked in his usual hit-and-run methods.	AA
	4/5 5		At 7am. Very heavy enemy barrage opened on our front line. Continued till 7.30 - trench mortars put down heavily shelled and for shells 4.2 & 18pdr & 77mm. At 8.50am enemy put opposite him by Lewis fire killed, about 10 enemy wounded, an attack on ESSEX & SUFFOLK positions - was reported. At 11.10 am Gunstaine Brigade on our right were attacked and enemy reported to be holding Pau - BERNACOURT - LAVEVILLE road. Left of 35th Brigade. Z & later day between us. Against 13th Brigade. SOS on our front was initiated and also on my right opposite Hill 35th Brigade.	AA
	6		Heavy shelling of our lines between AVELUY at 5am. SOS on our front two hundred yards.	AA

Army Form C. 2118.

WAR DIARY
or
INTELLIGENCE SUMMARY.
(Erase heading not required.)

Army: **76th Brigade. R.F.A.**
Month and year: **April 1916**
Ref: **M.A.P. FRANCE** Sheet **57 D S.E.**

Place	Date 1916	Hour	Summary of Events and Information	Remarks and references to Appendices
ENGELBELMER	April 7		Relief completed. Batteries ordered to HARPONVILLE, remaining in Corps Reserve until 12th inst.	A1
	12		After dusk batteries moved into "silent" positions in P.24 & P.29	A1
	13		Batteries commenced digging gun pits, trenches, ammunition recesses etc.	A1
	14		Work on positions carried on	
	15			A1
	16			
	17		Reserve positions in P.26 & P.32 for defence of ENGELBELMER & Lines reconnoitred.	A1
	18		ENGELBELMER purely heavily shelled during the day, about 200 rds. 4.2 fired into MATIN J.H.R.T	A1 A1 A1
	19		MESNIL & front line in B.29 b, d, were heavily shelled	
	20		E.A. very active during day and night. Enemy flight below normal	A1
	21		At 6.14 p.m. again at 6.50 p.m. & S.O.S. went up from MESNIL. Batteries fired on their S.O.S. lines action at 8 p.m. Our infantry fired on night or approaches in Q.35.b	
	22		Hostile shelling normal. ENGELBELMER & FORESVILLE were shelled during the day by 4.2. Visibility low. E.A. activity below normal	A1
	23		At 7 a.m. enemy attack took place to ferret portion of enemy's lines opp. Q.25. d & Q.35.c at 4 hour	

Army Form C. 2118.

WAR DIARY
or
INTELLIGENCE SUMMARY.
(Erase heading not required.)

7 8 Brigade R.F.A.

Place	Date	Hour	Summary of Events and Information	Remarks and references to Appendices
ENGLEBELMER	April 1916		Ref. MAP FRANCE SHEET 57d N.E.	
	22	4 hour	Batt: H.Q. am P.28.d. enemy heavily shelled L.4 & 2	1M
	23		Position P.19.a. re heavily shelled in bursts of fire during the evening.	2M
	24		Hammered to P.22.d. bombing. Hostile shelling below normal.	3M
	25		In the afternoon MESNIL was heavily shelled with 4.2 & 77 mm	4M
	26		MESNIL shelled with about 30 enemy gas shells	5M
	27		Left Brigade front on S.R. 3 Zone from 8.45 & 9.15 p.m. 10 rnds pr.	6M
			ranker. Right Brigade answer per E.O.S. shortage experienced	
			named at 9.15 p.m.	
	28		Hostile fire above normal. E.H. activity above normal. Enemy?	7M
			thought to be in GREEDY WOOD & MESNIL	
	29		73 star parts on on P.24.C. shelled during evening, also round	8M
			in 923 L. entire 4.2	
	30		Hostile fire below normal. Battery position in valley P.2.4 shelled	9M
			by A.2. during the evening.	
			Casualties Nil.	
			Casualties during month:- 1 Officer killed
			4 Officers wounded
			8 Other Ranks killed
			21 Other Ranks wounded

AWARDS:- Major W.F. Jennington. M.C. 26/4/18.
No. 72811 Corpl. L. Jones M.S.M. 26/4/18.
No. 11273 Cpl. J. Ban A. Gre. C/18. M.M. 26/4/18.
M. 74/6. Sergt. A. Croft. M.M. 26/4/18.
Sergt F. Bailow. M/15. M.M. 26/4/18.
Gunner H.J. Sept F. Bailow. M/15. M.M. 26/4/18.
Bdr. J. Lewis. M/15. M.M. 24/4/18.
Bdr. P. Rookery M/18. M.M. 24/4/18.
C.J. Landis Sjt A/R M/18. 24/4/18.
Sjt. H. Harding M/15-M.M. 24/4/18.

Ammunition expended.

A 429 AX 3703 BX 2262.

Vol 35

Army Form C. 2118.

WAR DIARY
or
INTELLIGENCE SUMMARY.
(Erase heading not required.)

MAY 1918   78 Brigade R.F.A.

REF: MAP. FRANCE. SHEET 57.d. S.E. 1:20,000

Place	Date MAY	Hour	Summary of Events and Information	Remarks and references to Appendices
ENGELBELMER	1		MESNIL & ENGELBELMER, shelled during the day. Aviation Nil.	MS
	2		MESNIL shelled with heavy shells during the day, also P24 & north about 3.0 am.th. E.A. active all day.	MS
	3		MARTINSART, WESTERN edge, & AVELUY heavily shelled. There was considerable aerial activity all day.	MS
	4		MESNIL shelled as usual all day. Bombs on P24c scored by 77 mm gun about 11 E.A. inspection over our lines during the day.	MS
	5		One section from each battery took up active positions in P36c. & Q31 & d. E.A. less active. Hoop Greatcoat carried out on MILL Q26.1.6	MS
	6		Registration carried out. Outskirts of ENGELBELMER Wood & Village about V12 & shelled during the day. Six Albatross Scouts patrolled in line but did not cross. Visibility good. Cooper Concentration usual night firing carried out.	MS
	7		ENGELBELMER Wood, X Roads in P23 d & W3 shelled during the day. Night firing & cooper concentration carried out. During the morning about 10 RUMPLER Scouts patrolled the front, & 8 ALBATROSS fighters over MESNIL ours down 9.	MS
	8		Hostile shelling below normal. Visibility good. Aerial activity below normal. Night firing on tracks, bridges & carried out.	MS

Army Form C. 2118.

WAR DIARY
or
INTELLIGENCE SUMMARY.
(Erase heading not required.) 76th Brigade. R.F.A.

Place	Date MAY	Hour	Summary of Events and Information REF. WAR FRANCE SHEET 57d S.E. 1:20,000	Remarks and references to Appendices
ENGEL BELMER	9		P.23 & P.24 heavily shelled between 6 pm & 11 pm by 5.9 & some 8". Enemy aerial activity above normal. Harassing fire throughout the night carried out on tracks, hedges etc.	AH
	10		MESNIL MARTINSART Valley shelled during the morning. Very little aerial activity. Brigade assisted in operation by 38th DIV: in overnight to advance our line in AVELUY WOOD. This was unsuccessful.	AH
	11		Hostile shelling above normal. ENGEL & BELMER - MARTINSART receiving most attention. Visibility poor. Aerial activity below normal.	AH
	12		Visibility poor. Hostile + own artillery fairly active. Usual night firing carried out.	AH
	13		Very little hostile shelling. Enemy transport on MIRAUMONT - BEAUCOURT Road most successfully engaged by 15pdrs: & 4.5 hows. Several damages being done & considerable confusion caused by direct hits.	AH
	14		Hostile artillery active. HEDAUVILLE - PUZENNES heavily shelled in the morning. Aerial activity above normal. Visibility very good.	AH

Army Form C. 2118.

WAR DIARY
or
INTELLIGENCE SUMMARY.

(Erase heading not required.)

MAY 1918 Ref. MAP. FRANCE 7 8 Brigade. R.F.A.

Instructions regarding War Diaries and Intelligence Summaries are contained in F. S. Regs., Part II. and the Staff Manual respectively. Title pages will be prepared in manuscript.

Place	Date MAY	Hour	Summary of Events and Information SHEET. 57d. S.E. 1:20,000	Remarks and references to Appendices
ENGELBELMER	15		ENGELBELMER intermittently shelled during the day with 5.9 + 4.2 & a few 77 m/m. Visibility very poor in the morning & fork in the evening. Night firing carried out as usual.	AWS
	16		MESNIL shelled during the afternoon. MARTINSART & hamels & ENGELBELMER shelled by 77 m/m from direction of THIEPVAL WOOD. Enemy aerial activity below normal, no planes active. Registration carried out.	AWS
	17		Visibility good. Intermittent shelling of P.24.e in the morning by 4.1 form. Q.31.b shelled by 4.2 & 5.9 for half during the evening. Registration carried out by all active forms, aerial activity but increased considerably in the afternoon. Movement in Q.24.a was engaged by 4.5 how with good results.	AWS
	18		From 11 pm the previous evening till 4 am this morning, the area in P.36.b.c.d + V.6.a were heavily shelled with 8" 5.9 - 4.2 & 77 m/m with considerable proportion of gas. At 12.15 am a raid was successfully carried out by the Brigade on our left in which our batteries cooperated. Few casualties, few prisoners taken & heavy enemy acknowledged by 317th Brigade.	AWS
	19			AWS

Army Form C. 2118.

WAR DIARY
or
INTELLIGENCE SUMMARY.

(Erase heading not required.) 78th Brigade. R.F.A

Place	Date	Hour	Summary of Events and Information	Remarks and references to Appendices
ENGELBELMER	MAY 1918.		Ref: MAP. FRANCE SHEET 57 d. S.E. 1: 20,000	
	19	continued	At 10.28 pm heavy firing reported on our front & batteries opened on general bombardment. At 10.34 pm. S.O.S reported from no 1 on heavy fire & up between night + Centre Brigades & batteries answered to S.O.S rate of fire. till 10.50 pm when all reported quiet. It subsequently transpired that the enemy had successfully raided line of our posts.	SAB
	20		Between 12.30 am & 1pm enemy in P24c & a P30a were heavily shelled by 4.2 & 5.9 from direction of THIEPVAL WOOD. Wireless Section reported early in the morning that they had picked up the information that enemy in P24 b & d & P30 b & d were to be relieved during the day by the enemy. Relief of brigade completed by 11.30am & batteries remained at wagon lines in Corps Mobile Reserve.	NK
	21st/24		Remained in Corps Mobile Reserve.	
	25.		Batteries each returned in section of 93rd Brigade in positions round MAILLY-MAILLET & VITERMONT.	
	26		Relief completed.	

Army Form C. 2118.

WAR DIARY
or
INTELLIGENCE SUMMARY.

(Erase heading not required.)   78th BRIGADE. R.F.A.

Instructions regarding War Diaries and Intelligence Summaries are contained in F.S. Regs., Part II. and the Staff Manual respectively. Title pages will be prepared in manuscript.

MAY 1918   REF. MAP. FRANCE   SHEET 57d. S.E. 1:20,000

Place	Date	Hour	Summary of Events and Information	Remarks and references to Appendices
BEAUSART ENGELBELMER	27.	2 am to 4.30 am	Heavy general bombardment of front line whole divn, most intense between 3.30 & 5.30 on 63rd Divn. front on our right. Heavy T.M. bombardment of our line at 9.15 am. 3.30 pm, hrs of fire on BEAUSART - MAILLY MAILLET ROAD at 3.30 pm & again at 6 pm. Night firing carried out as ordered.	AWS
	28.		Visibility good. 10.30 am some hostile mobile machines engaged by our planes & driven off. P.12.C. Shelling positive shelled with 4.2 hows at 10 am & again at 1.25 pm. At 2 pm 11" Naval gun fired a few rounds on P.17 & at long intervals after 5.0 pm. Heavy T.M. bombardment of front line reported. Forward Arm. replied with 20 rounds on L.S. Lines. Between 10 pm & 12 pm P.18.C. & Q.13.C. Shelled with 5.9, 4.2 + fives. Aerial activity normal. Forward Arm. carried out registration. Visibility good. Night firing carried out.	AWS
	29.		Visibility poor. LEALVILLERS. Shelled at intervals during the morning by long range 11" gun (H.V.) Aerial activity below normal. Night general.	AWS
	30.		Visibility good. Planes on both sides active - hostile shelling during the day below normal.	AWS

Army Form C. 2118.

WAR DIARY
or
INTELLIGENCE SUMMARY.

78th BRIGADE. R.F.A.

(Erase heading not required.)

Title pages MAY 1918

Place	Date	Hour	Summary of Events and Information REF. MAP FRANCE SHEET 57 D.S.E. 1:20,000	Remarks and references to Appendices
BEAUSART ENGELBELMER	30		continued. 7 pm to 9 pm 60 rounds 4.2 on MAILLY MAILLET — BEAUSART ROAD, short observed by 2 F.A. Night firing + corps concentration carried out as ordered.	MS
	31.		Throughout the morning 18pdrs: fired shrapnel at intervals on BEAUSART. Hostile shoot took place on front support lines about 6.30 pm. Night firing as ordered.

Ammunition Expended:-
A   AX   BX   BHC   BSS
9402 2565 2085 469   650

Casualties:- 3 Officers (Gas Effects).
23 O.R. (Gas Effect)
3 OR Wounded
3 OR Killed.

Awards:- Nr. 7025 Driver Woodcock J. (B/78) M.M. M.G.27/18. | MS |

B.K. Strand Capt RHA
for O.C. 78 Brigade RHA

Army Form C. 2118.

VOL 36

WAR DIARY
or
INTELLIGENCE SUMMARY.

(Erase heading not required.)

Instructions regarding War Diaries and Intelligence Summaries are contained in F. S. Regs., Part II. and the Staff Manual respectively. Title pages will be prepared in manuscript.

JUNE 1916   REF. MAP. FRANCE   78th BRIGADE. R.F.A.   SHEET 57.d. S.E. 1:20,000

Place	Date Hour	Summary of Events and Information	Remarks and references to Appendices
BEAUSART ENGELBELMER	1	Chinese barrage party by brigade on Q4d, in cooperation with operation being carried out by 35th DIV: to recapture S.W. portion of AVELUY WOOD. Our front remained quiet. This operation was partly successful to starboard, but front found could not be held. Between 3.30 & 4 p.m. front line heavily strafed mortared — no hows retaliation. 9.45 to 10.30 p.m. area shot on P10b & P11b also P15a.b.c.&.D. Night firing carried out as ordered. Visibility in evening too heavy for aerial observation — improving later.	SHS
	2	2 a.m. to 3 a.m. about 250 rounds fell on P15&6 &d, all calibres — some gas. Night was quiet on this front.	SHS
	3rd to 5th	Normal Trench warfare. Hostile shelling normal. Fwd Conc Concentration harassing fire on communication trenches, roads & back.	SHS
	6	Day quiet. At 10.5 p.m. our batteries put down a creeping barrage in cooperation with an infantry raid by two battalions on enemy system on Y. Ravine which was a complete success.	SHS
	9-14	Enemy Arty. May was more active firing a considerable number of concentrations on roads & tracks in back areas.	SHS

Army Form C. 2118.

WAR DIARY
or
INTELLIGENCE SUMMARY.

(Erase heading not required.) 78th Brigade, R.F.A.

Instructions regarding War Diaries and Intelligence Summaries are contained in F.S. Regs., Part II. and the Staff Manual respectively. Title pages will be prepared in manuscript.

Place	Date	Hour	Summary of Events and Information	Remarks and references to Appendices
BEAU AND JUNE 1918			REF. MAP. FRANCE SHEET 57A. S.E. 1:20,000	
ENCELAR	15-19		Situation normal. Usual harassing fire carried out. Enemy artillery very quiet except on night of 18th when a heavy mustard gas bombardment of our A, B, & D batteries took place.	WE
	20		Day quiet on the whole with exception of some shelling of C & D and front-line systems. During the night a successful Projector attack was carried out - in 4.5 comprised with fire & 18 pdr fired shrapnel in conjunction.	WE
	21-24		Usual times amongst. Gas projector attack repeated	WE WE
	25		One section two battery was relieved by 223rd Bde = 63 (R.N.) Div.	WE
	26		Relief completed. Brigade moved into corps Reserve as G.H.Q & Corps mobile Reserve.	WE
	30		78th Brigade & 79th Brigade moved into camp in neighbourhood of DAOURS, having been lent to 4th Australian Corps.
Ammunition expended } A 1316.4. A x 5220. B x oo 6703.
Casualties 3 officers wounded F & R wounded. gas
J.H. Stinton
for O.C. 78 Bde R.F.A.	WE

D.D. & L. London, E.C. (A'coy.) Wt. W41727/M2031 750,000 5/17 Sch. 32 Forms C2.9/14

Army Form C. 2118.

WAR DIARY
or
INTELLIGENCE SUMMARY.
(Erase heading not required.)

7 8 A Brigade. R.F.A.

Place	Date JULY	Hour	Summary of Events and Information Ref: MAP FRANCE SHEET 62 D. N.E. 1:20,000	Remarks and references to Appendices
CORBIE	1		July. 1918. After nightfall march Brigade arrived at Wryn Wood in VECQUEMONT area. a reconnaissance of battery positions in the morning & Batteries & HAMLET moved into positions during the evening. Positions to remain silent.	AHS
	2		Only a few rounds were allowed per battery for registration. During the night enemy very active with harassing fire & three batteries had slight casualties.	AHS
	3		Enemy fire below normal during day. Enemy S.O.S.	AHS
	4		At 3.10 a.m. our artillery opened & the Australian Infantry supported by 2 battalions of Americans & 46 tanks attacked. Slight resistance offered & hostile barrage poor. Attack apparently a complete surprise. All objectives were gained. 35 Officers (a Battn. HQ Staff) + 13 or more men were taken, 2 Field guns, 100 m.g. & 14 T.M. During the early part of the day, enemy bombarded HAMEL cross roads from line h.6.5 north & were very erratic, & our H.A. carried out good counter battery shoots.	AHS

Army Form C. 2118.

WAR DIARY
or
INTELLIGENCE SUMMARY.
(Erase heading not required.)

Place: JULY 1918

Date	Hour	Summary of Events and Information REF. MAP. FRANCE SHEET 62 d N.E. 1:20,000 75th Brigade. R.F.A.	Remarks and references to Appendices
July 4		(contind) at 10.20 p.m. enemy counter attacked in pln, taking 11 prisoners. Australians immediately attacked recovering their prisoners & taking 50 more.	AN
5		Day quiet. Batteries pulled out in the evening switching to their W.L.	AN
6	10pm	Brigade marched back to its Wagon Lines in LEALVILLERS area & remained in G.H.Q. & Corps Mobile Reserve	AN
12		Orders received to relieve 12th D.A. (63rd Bde) in the AVELUY sector, batteries went in to positions during the night	AN
13		Visibility good. Hostile fire below normal. Harassing fire carried out during the night into enemy approaches ANCRE to AVELUY &c.	AN
14		Harassing fire kept up throughout day & night on various points.	AN

Army Form C. 2118.

WAR DIARY
or
INTELLIGENCE SUMMARY.
(Erase heading not required.)

78th Brigade. R.F.A.

JULY 1916

REF. MAP. FRANCE SHEET 57 d.S.E. 1:20,000

Place	Date July	Hour	Summary of Events and Information	Remarks and references to Appendices
SENLIS	15		Usual harassing fire carried out. 5175 fired 10 min: fm ammunition	SWA
	16		Visibility fair. E.A. very active – 1 enemy balloon brought down	SWA
	17		Nothing to report	SWA
	18		38th Div. withdrawn & V Corps held by 2 divisions – 17th Div: extending its line as far North as MESNIL (incl) with 3 Brigades on the line & no battalions in each in front line –	SWA
	19/21		Nothing to report-	SWA
	22		Daylight raid carried out by 10th W. YORKS. 1 prisoner taken	SWA
	23		Considerable movement observed during the day on roads on X19a & W24 c.d, probably enemy relief in daylight - Engaged with good results by HA	SWA
	24		Raid by 47th Div: on right. No identifications	SWA
	25/27		Nothing to report.	SWA

Army Form C. 2118.

WAR DIARY
or
INTELLIGENCE SUMMARY.

(Erase heading not required.)

78th Brigade. R.F.A.

Instructions regarding War Diaries and Intelligence Summaries are contained in F. S. Regs., Part II. and the Staff Manual respectively. Title pages will be prepared in manuscript.

JULY 1918

REF. MAP. FRANCE. SHEET 57d S.E. 1:20,000

Place	Date July	Hour	Summary of Events and Information	Remarks and references to Appendices
SENLIS.	28		Heavy Shelling throughout night, moving on SENLIS. Weather bad. Visibility variable.	JMS
	29		Expenditure on day & night harassing fire doubled	JMS
	30		At 9.25 am a bombardment was carried out all on field & M.A. on the Corps front. Smoke screens were put down. No enemy retaliation for 7 minutes, when our CTs & BOUZINCOURT were fairly heavily shelled. At 9.55 am fire was repeated for 3 minutes. Enemy retaliated slightly on back areas. Remainder of day quiet.	JMS
	31.		Visibility poor early but improved later. Large exploitation over Scott & ALBERT at about 10 p.m., continued to hum for some time. Casualties :— 1 - OR drowned 7 - OR wounded	JMS
			Ammunition Expended :— A 1232 S AX 678 ASS 483 BX 8479 BCG 766 BNC6 BSS 32	

Signed,
for OC 78. Brigade. R.F.A.

17th Divl.
Artillery

78th BRIGADE.

ROYAL FIELD ARTILLERY,

AUGUST 1918.

24

WAR DIARY
or
INTELLIGENCE SUMMARY

(Erase heading not required)

Army Form C. 2118.

WD 38

78th Brigade. R.F.A.

Place	Date Aug.	Hour	Summary of Events and Information Ref. "MAP. FRANCE. Sheet 57 D S.E. 1:20,000	Remarks and references to Appendices
SENLIS	1		50th Infantry Bde. carried out successful raid, capturing 16 men + 2 M.G.	NIL
	2		The 76th Bde: assisted with a box barrage.	NIL
	3		Nothing of interest to report.	NIL
			Patrols which had gone out over night found the enemy had withdrawn across the ANCRE. After moving dug outs + blowing up bridges + crossings.	NIL
	4		B.C.s reconnoitred Battery positions about 400 yds of the ANCRE – engaged movement in X 13 + X 17.	NIL
	5		One section per battery of 78th Brigade returned by 121st Bde. 38th S.A.	NIL
	6		Relief completed + Brigade went to W.L. in G.H.Q Reserve, at VARENNES.	NIL
	8		Brigade marched to BLANGY TRONVILLE in 4th Army Area.	NIL
	9		Orders received to march to CORBIE after 8 pm.	NIL
	12		17th D.V. relieve the 3rd Australian Div. Artillery in action near MORCOURT.	NIL
MORCOURT	13 mid.		Considerable bombing of village + back area. Enemy artillery active with heavy hostile H.A. assembly positions.	NIL
	15		Our Infantry unsuccessfully tried to establish post in ridge E of MERICOURT, with artillery co-operation	NIL

Army Form C. 2118.

WAR DIARY
or
INTELLIGENCE SUMMARY.
(Erase heading not required.)

78th Bde; R.F.A.

Place	Date Aug	Hour	Summary of Events and Information	Remarks and references to Appendices
MORCOURT	16		Reg: MAP FRANCE 1:20,000. Nothing to report. Relieved by 5th Australian Div; & Brigade marched to wagon lines at VECQUEMONT.	AW1
	17			AW1 / JHS
	19		Bde. march into old wagon lines on V. Corprone near VARENNES.	AW1 / JHS
	20		Battery positions reconnoitred N. of MESNIL & battery went into action after dark in MESNIL VALLEY.	AW1
MESNIL	21/22/23		Nothing to report.	
	24		1 Section per battery moved forward across the ANCRE & took up positions off THIEPVAL ROAD. During the morning, 1 gun under MAJOR MARSHALL D.S.O. M.C. accompanied the 9th E. YORKS. Regt. in their advance on POZIERES. This battalion was held up by M.G. fire at — MOUET FARM, & the gun of 9/78 was brought into action on the front line & fired point blank range, effectively silencing the M.G.s one after another & causing considerable consternation on the enemy, & enabling the Infantry to capture POZIERES. Later in the afternoon the enemy massed for a strong counter attack; this gun was again brought into action in the front line marks & fired over open sights under very heavy shell & M.G. fire, a very bright assisted in halting of the attack. 78/78 & 19/78 cooperated in the advance of the MANCHESTERS with forward Sections	AW1
	25			

WAR DIARY or INTELLIGENCE SUMMARY

Army Form C. 2118.

(Erase heading not required.)

Reg: MAR. FRANCE 78th Bde; R.F.A.
SHEET 57 D.S.E.

Place	Date Aug	Hour	Summary of Events and Information	Remarks and references to Appendices
COURCELETTE	25	1.20 am	Remaining guns carried to ANCRE & took up position near COURCELETTE. A/78 with a forward gun, in the morning, assisted the Lancashire Fusiliers in their advance, firing again over open sights & causing heavy enemy casualties. In the afternoon this gun & the forward actions of B/78 & D/78 were largely instrumental in repelling a strong counter attack from N of HIGH WOOD.	AHS
	26		Enemy reported to be retiring E of FLERS, so B/78 & D/78 came forward behind HIGH WOOD, remaining batteries took up positions in front of MARTINPUISH. During the evening the 50th Infantry Bde: passed thro' 51st & 52nd Brigade and entered FLERS on the line. During the night the 51st Brigade attacked but met with little success.	AHS
	27		In the morning enemy counter-attacked FLERS & made some progress. At 6am JD ords repeated in FLERS, SOS was almost at once received & batteries opened on S.O.S. lines E of the village, stopping firing at 7 am.	AHS
	28		At 5.15 am enemy started counter preparation which ceased at 6 am, nothing further of interest occurred	AHS

Army Form C. 2118.

WAR DIARY
or
INTELLIGENCE SUMMARY.
(Erase heading not required.)

Ref: MAP. FRANCE. 78 & B di: R.7.A
SHEET. 57 D. S. E 1. 20,000.

Place	Date Aug	Hour	Summary of Events and Information	Remarks and references to Appendices
MARTINPUICH	29		At 5:15 am Enemy attacked 38th Div: on our right attacked — objectives LONGUEVAL & DELVE WOOD. His was completely successful enemy withdrew rapidly towards LE TRANSLOY during the morning. Battery advanced & took up position EAST OF FLERS with forward section — one gun in forward being pushed forward to closely support the Infantry.	NIL
FLERS	30		So/enemy Lit up by machine gun fire about 1500 yards W. of LE TRANSLOY. Battery moved forward to their forward section early in the morning & later section from B/78 & C/78 advanced with the valley W of LESBOEUFS.	NIL
	31		Nothing to report. Enemy shelling in back areas.	NIL

Ammunition A 15284. A×7341
Expended   B× 7852

Casualties. 4 Officers Wounded
3. O.Rs. Killed
19. O.Rs. Wounded

S.H. Shand. Cpr.
for O.C. 78th Bde: R.7.A

Army Form C. 2118.

Vol 39

WAR DIARY
or
INTELLIGENCE SUMMARY.
(Erase heading not required.)

78th Brigade. R.F.A.

Instructions regarding War Diaries and Intelligence Summaries are contained in F.S. Regs., Part II. and the Staff Manual respectively. Title pages will be prepared in manuscript.

Place	Date Sept	Hour	Summary of Events and Information SHEET 57C S.W. 1.20.000	Remarks and references to Appendices
LES BOEUFS	1		Sep. 1st 1918. Rg: Maj. FRANCE. Joint attack at 5:40 a.m. with artillery support by 17th DIV: 21st DIV. 38th DIV. 52nd Infantry Brigade objective – Line E of LE TRANSLOY. Attack was unsuccessful & line remained unchanged.	AHS
	2		The same three Div: again attacked at 5 am with artillery support were partially successful. The 17th Div: were nr the main BAPAUME-PERONNE road by 10 am – isolated parties of the enemy were still in Southern part of village & hampered the advance. 18 pdr: Batteries moved their main postns up to their forward sectns during the morning. 38th Div: reported in SAILLY SAILLISEL & enemy retiring E of ROCQUIGNY.	AHS
	3		Batteries moved forward to valley behind ROCQUIGNY. At 10 am a section of A/176 with an escort of 1 Coy LANCS: FUSILIERS was sent forward to occupy Windu Farm a high found in neighborhood. This was successfully accomplished by 1pm. In the afternoon batteries moved forward to postns to capture YTRES – EQUINCOURT System South of B.O.S. Infantry advanced but were held up by machine gun fire.	AHS
	4		42nd Div: on the left reported taking line disposally across P.22 & New Zealand for part of HAVRINCOURT WOOD.	AHS
	5		Infantry attacked to capture trenches in P.34 & V.4 at 9 am with artillery support – enemy showed little resistance attack was successful.	AHS
	6		Allow a quiet night A/176. C/176. D/178 moved forward across CANAL DU NORD to positions in valley nr P.33.v.3 about 1000 x w of EQUINCOURT-YTRES System	AHS

Army Form C. 2118.

WAR DIARY
or
INTELLIGENCE SUMMARY.

(Erase heading not required.) 78th Brigade. R.F.A.

Instructions regarding War Diaries and Intelligence Summaries are contained in F.S. Regs., Part II. and the Staff Manual respectively. Title pages will be prepared in manuscript.

Place	Date Sept	Hour	Summary of Events and Information SHEET 57 c S.W. 1:20,000. REF. MAP: FRANCE	Remarks and references to Appendices
FINS	7		Sept 1918. Battery moved forward to valley N of FINS	AHS
	8		Situation unchanged	AHS
	9		New Zealand Div: attacked at 11 am to establish defensive system west of GOOZENCOURT in order to support barrage. 17th Div: Artillery assisted. The objective was not all gained.	AHS
	10		Situation unchanged. One section J.3/78 – 9/78 moved forward to positions N of DESSART WOOD.	AHS
	11		Infantry had orders to consolidate on line in HEATHER SUPPORT TRESCAULT RIDGE. The remaining guns J.3/78 + 9/78 joined the advanced sections.	AHS
	12		At 5.45 fired barrage in support of attack by N. Zealand Div: on TRESCAULT RIDGE. This was only partially successful – objective on N.Z. left being gained, but practically no progress on right.	AHS
	13		At 9.50 am enemy opened fairly heavy bombardment on our front & a heavier concentration on Div: on our right. At 9.55 opened SOS on our front & fire on S.O.S lines & at 10.5 concentrated all fire on right of Div: front. It transpired that enemy had come over from at 10.25 ceased firing. It transpired that enemy had come over from CHAPEL HILL but did not reach our trenches, being repulsed by machine gun fire – He left a few dead & wounded & some prisoners were taken. At dark A/78 + D/78 moved forward to positions in W.26 & 31 c respectively North of DESSART WOOD. About 10 pm 2 enemy bombing planes were brought down in flames by A.A. fire	AHS

Army Form C. 2118.

WAR DIARY
or
INTELLIGENCE SUMMARY.

78th Brigade. R.F.A.

(Erase heading not required.)

Instructions regarding War Diaries and Intelligence Summaries are contained in F. S. Regs., Part II. and the Staff Manual respectively. Title pages will be prepared in manuscript.

Place	Date Sept 1918	Hour	Summary of Events and Information SHEET 57c. S.E. 1:20,000	Remarks and references to Appendices
FINS	14		Ref. MAP. FRANCE Nothing to report	AWB
	15		N. portion of DESSART WOOD & neighbourhood shelled intermittently during the night with gas & H.E. Reconnaissance patrols fm 93rd A.F.A.B.	AWB
	16		Positions of batteries shelled fairly heavily during the night with H.E. & gas.	AWB
	17		Nothing to report.	
	18		Heavy fire slackening during early hours of the morning of battery positions & DESSART WOOD, followed by heavy H.E. barrage at 4.30 am. 36th Div: attacked with artillery support in conjunction with 17th Div: on right — 5th Div: on left, to capture high ground round GOUZEAUCOURT — Right brigade of 36th Div: gained their objective, but left Brigade held up in AFRICAN TRENCH — 17th Div: gained all objectives — 5th Div: made no progress. At 9 pm 36th Div: attacked in conjunction with 17th Div: but made no progress.	AWB
	19		17th Div: reports holding QUENTIN REDOUBT & forming line up round railway & LANCASHIRE TRENCH	AWB

Army Form C. 2118.

WAR DIARY
or
INTELLIGENCE SUMMARY.
(Erase heading not required.)

78th Brigade R.F.A.

Instructions regarding War Diaries and Intelligence Summaries are contained in F.S. Regs., Part II. and the Staff Manual respectively. Title pages will be prepared in manuscript.

Place	Date Sept 1918	Hour	Summary of Events and Information REF. MAP FRANCE SHEET 57c S.E. 1/20,000.	Remarks and references to Appendices
FINS	20		Enemy bombarded front line system heavily 6.45 - 7.0 p.m. No infy. action followed. DESSART WOOD shelled intermittently during the night. 17th Div (50th, 52nd Bdes) relieved 38th Div. in the line.	AM
"	21		Nothing to report	AM
"	22		ditto	AM
"	23		'K' Special Coy RE projected gas at 1.30am & 4.0 am. On W. side of GOUZEAUCOURT. Bde fired in conjunction.	AM
"	24		New Battery Position in N.9.10 & 11. N. of HEUDECOURT reconnoitred.	AM
"	25		K Special Coy RE projected gas at 3.0 am & 4.30 am W. side of GOUZEAUCOURT. Batteries fired in conjunction. HQ & Batteries occupied new positions N. of HEUDECOURT. 21st Infy. relieved 17th Div. Infy. 21st DA took over from 17th DA.	AM
HEUDECOURT	26		Nothing to report.	AM
"	27		At 7.52 am 62nd Infy. Bde attacked AFRICAN TRENCH in conjunction with an attack on the left by 5th Divn. 78th Bde RFA smoke screened left. Ground in R.26. Attack successful but driven out later by counter attack.	AM

WAR DIARY
or
INTELLIGENCE SUMMARY.

Army Form C. 2118.

78 Brigade RFA

REF MAP FRANCE SHEET 57°SE 1/20,000

Place	Date	Hour	Summary of Events and Information	Remarks and references to Appendices
GOUZEAUCOURT	Sept 28 1918		Patrols found GOUZEAUCOURT empty. HQ + Batteries moved to positions W.B. Rly. S.E. GOUZEAUCOURT. At 3.30am Bde supported attack by 110th Inf Bde in conjunction with 5th Dn on left & 33rd Dn on right for TRENCH SYSTEM R34 c+d - VILLERS GUISLAIN ROAD through R33 a+c & X3a 2nd objective TRENCH SYSTEM R34 c+d X5 a+c. Infy reached GOUZEAUCOURT - VILLERS GUISLAIN line R31 a - X2 a+b & X3c. 9 later TRENCH LINE through R32 c+d	Ann.
do.	29		Nothing to report	Ann.
GONNELIEU	30		Patrols found GONNELIEU unoccupied & infy occupied TRENCH SYSTEM R3 u c+d. Bttys moved into positions N.E. of GONNELIEU. Addenda. The Bde. fired dummy creeping barrage moving N.E. from N.E. corner of GONNELIEU at 2.45am 30th in support of operations on our left. Casualties Killed — 1 Officer + 5 O Ranks Wounded — 3 Officers + 36 O Ranks — 24 O Ranks — (Gas) Amm. Expended. — A.15 798A x 5657A/d 1256 Bac 415 855 398	Ann.

R.Rose Lt Col
Comdg 78 Bde RFA

Army Form C. 2118

WAR DIARY
or
INTELLIGENCE SUMMARY
(Erase heading not required.)

78 Bde RFA

Vol 40

Instructions regarding War Diaries and Intelligence Summaries are contained in F.S. Regs., Part II. and the Staff Manual respectively. Title Pages will be prepared in manuscript.

Place	Date Oct. 1918	Hour	Summary of Events and Information. SHEETS 57°SE & 57 B SW. REF MAP FRANCE	Remarks and references to Appendices
GONNELIEU	1		Nothing to report.	AM.
do.	2		CRA 21st Div. Arty. visited Bty. Positions. B/78 moved a Section up to — QUARRY POST R29d.	AM.
do.	3		Quiet. Nothing to report.	AM.
do.	4		CRA 21st D.A. visited position. D/78 moved a Section to near QUARRY POST. Quiet.	AM.
do.	5		Enemy withdrew. Infy occupied HINDENBURG LINE from BANTOUZELLE & RONCOURT FARM. Patrols pushed through VAUCELLES WOOD, RANCOURT COPSE. Bde HQ moved to BANTEUX. RE's completed bridge across CANAL at BANTEUX at 19.30 hrs. D/78 & 1 Section C/78 moved across CANAL.	AM.
VAUCELLES WOOD	6		All Batteries in action in M35 c&d. by 6.0 am. Bde HQ in Enemy 8" How position M34d05. Infy occupied part of BEAUREVOIR LINE.	AM.
	7		Quiet. Spot sniping done by batteries on enemy at MIDDLE and MALASSISE COPSES.	AM.
	8		Infy attacked at 01.00 hr in Easterly direction to take HAUT FARM and ANGLES CH^AU. Successful. At 05.15 hr. Infy attacked again in Northerly direction from Line of E&W. ROAD past ANGLES CH^AU to line MEZIERES COPSE – HURTEBIS FARM. At 06.30 hrs. A C & D Batteries moved into position in N25 b+c. to cover new attack East from Line HURTEBIS FARM – ARDISSART FARM – ANGLES CH^AU at 08.00 hrs. Infy advanced to line	AM.

Army Form C. 2118

WAR DIARY
or
INTELLIGENCE SUMMARY

(Erase heading not required.)

78 Bde R.F.A.

Summary of Events and Information SHEETS 57 B SW 9 57 B NE

REF. MAP FRANCE.

Place	Date	Hour	Summary of Events and Information	Remarks and references to Appendices
VAUCELLES WOOD	8 (cont.) 1918		Line of HURTEBIS COPSE. Bde HQ moved into WOOD M38c & later to near MEZIERES FARM. Batteries moved up to N20a & 26c. C/78 brought a section into half-cock position in M21c. 18 pdrs. did good work in chasing over 100 Bosche out of WALINCOURT TRENCH LINE back into WALINCOURT VILLAGE. D/78 knocked out an enemy M.G. in lodge by GUILLEMIN FARM which was holding up our infantry. Many good targets engaged.	A.M.M
SELVIGNY and CAULLERY	9.		17 Div. Infy. relieved 21st Div. Infy. 51st Infy. Bde. paraded in open capturing SELVIGNY and CAULLERY. Batteries in action E. of SELVIGNY and later in Q9a & 15d. B/78 ran a single gun into the open near PIERRE MILL relieved 2 enemy MGs firing from CLARY & MONTIGNY at our infy. This gun was put out of action by an enemy 7.7 gun firing over open sights from TRONQUOY. Bde HQ at CAULLERY. A & D/78 moved to Q4c. Infy. pushed through CLARY & MONTIGNY in the evening. Orders received from CRA. 21st Div. Arty. No congratulations.	A.M.M
LIGNY and INCHY	10		Advance continued by 50 Infy Bde. through AUDENCOURT BEAUMONT and INCHY to Western outskirts of NEUVILLY. 1 Section of D/78 in action in K18c at 0830 hrs. Rest of D & B Btys. in action 0845 hrs. Guns engaged enemy 77 gun firing over open sights.	A.M.M

WAR DIARY or INTELLIGENCE SUMMARY

Army Form C. 2118

78 Bde RFA

REF. MAP FRANCE SHEET 57B NE.

Place	Date Oct. 1918	Hour	Summary of Events and Information	Remarks and references to Appendices
INCHY	10 (cont.)		from aeroplane shd K 2 L and later Kleaves. Many good enemy infantry targets engaged. Enemy was holding VILLAGE (NEUVILLY) and Railway in strength. All Batteries in action J.17.a.23. R de HQ at INCHY. LEFT COY. got across Rly but had to withdraw any to bank of cutbank.	A.M. A.M.
do.	11		Quiet. Enemy shelled INCHY at night - not heavily. Active harassing fire carried out.	
do.	12		52nd Infy Bde. attacked at 05.00 hrs to take AMERVAL and HIGH GROUND N. and N.W. of it. Manchesters penetrated to line of ROAD through E 26.c and K 2.b. Right did not get on. Enemy in strength in NEUVILLY + along Rly. Manchesters withdrawn final line at end of day, along the W. bank of RIVER. Very active harassing fire carried out.	A.M. A.M.
do.	13		51st Infy Bde. relieved 52nd Infy Bde. in the line. Harassing fire continued.	A.M.
	14		Quiet morning. On learning fire kept up. Infy patrols sent out to Rly in afternoon	A.M.
	15-19		Nothing to report.	
	20		At 02.00 hrs 50th Infy Bde supported by 78. 79. 94. 94 and 34 Bdes RFA attacked + took NEUVILLY. The 51st Infy Bde passed through them and took AMERVAL & RIDGE. Batteries moved to positions S. of NEUVILLY	A.M.

Army Form C. 2118

WAR DIARY
or
INTELLIGENCE SUMMARY
(Erase heading not required.)

78 Bde RFA

Place	Date Oct 1918	Hour	Summary of Events and Information REF. MAP FRANCE SHEET 57 B NE & 57 A S.E.	Remarks and references to Appendices
NEUVILLY	21		52nd Infy Bde relieved 51st Infy Bde in the line. 78 Bde HQ moved into NEUVILLY.	AM
do.	22		Batteries moved across RIVER SELLE to positions S.E. of NEUVILLY. 21st Division relieved 17th. CRA 21st took over Arty Command.	AM
do.	23		At 02.00 hrs Bde. supported attack by 110 & 64 Infy Bdes in conjunction with whole of 3rd & 4th Armies. 78 Bde fired barrage up to VENDEGIES au BOIS. 64 Bde RFA followed through with 62 Infy Bde. Found Infy line ROAD NW. & SE through F 8 d. Batteries in action NE. of OVILLERS.	AM
OVILLERS	24		Bde fired barrage at 04.00 hrs. Supporting 62 & 64 Infy Bdes to line of ROAD from F 30.4.5 — F 10.4.D. Bde marched to positions E. of QUEDESNES and Later to positions W. of POIX du NORD. Bde fired barrage at 16.00 hrs. supporting 62 & 64 Infy Bdes to 2nd Objective — (57 A S.E.) ROAD X 24 a — 18 c — 17 d a.b — 11 c.9 a. Successful. At 13.00 hrs C/78 took a single gun up to X 28 a 8.8	
POIX du NORD	25		Nothing to report. 4 Bdes. used good shooting at M.G's & during the barrage at 16.00 hrs. sniped the enemy on their retreat.	AM
POIX du NORD	25		Half to aft. Batteries moved to positions in X 21 c + 28 a.	AM

Army Form C. 2118

WAR DIARY or INTELLIGENCE SUMMARY

(Erase heading not required.)

78 Bde R.F.A.

Place	Date Oct 1918	Hour	Summary of Events and Information	Remarks and references to Appendices
Poix du Nord	26		Ref. MAP FRANCE SHEET 57 NE & 57 A S.E.	
		at 01:00 hrs	Bde fired barrage to support Infy establishing posts on a line S13.d 4.3 – X11.b 3.8 in conjunction with an attack by 33rd Div. on the right. B/78 moved a section up to X16a 2.4. 52nd Infy Bde relieves 110 Infy Bde in the Line. 17th Div & 17 C.R.A. relieved 21 & 78 Bdes C.R.A. under the tactical command 9 52 Infy Bde in case Bde found move.	App.
	27		Nil	App.
	28		Nil	App.
	29		21st Infy & R.A. relieves 17th	App.
	30		78 Bde withdrew personnel to rest in Wagon Lines round VENDEGIES.	App.
	31		Nothing to report.	App.
	1st to 31st		Killed — 2 Officers — 5 Other Ranks
Wounded — 1 Officer — 62 Other Ranks
Wounded (Gas) — Officers — 8 Other Ranks

Ammunition Expended:—

A	AX	AS	ABB	AT
24536	10105	985	200	32

BX	BSS
8285	200
App.

J.C. Strudwick Major R.F.A.
for O.C. 78 Brigade R.F.A.

2/11/18

Army Form C. 2118

WAR DIARY or INTELLIGENCE SUMMARY

BELGIUM, PART OF FRANCE
REF. SHEET 51. 1:40,000.

78 Bde R.F.A.

Place	Date Nov 1918	Hour	Summary of Events and Information	Remarks and references to Appendices
POIX-du-NORD	1st		Nothing to Report. Brinne at Positions made up to for Res. R & R 10 PDR. 400 " " 4.5 How	29/1
"	2nd		" "	19/1
"	3rd		Bde. re-occupied positions	19/1
"	4th	04.00	Attack resumed by 17 Div. 78 Bde. put down creeping barrage in support from 04.00 hrs to 11.00 hrs. B/78 sent forward 1 section at 05.20 hrs for close support of INF. in successive objections. (O.C. B/78 & B/78 was forward to reconnoitre positions in support of the attack.)	19/1
		09.30	LINE RGAP T.20d.1.0. — T.9.C.3.0.	
		11.00	Bde. moved forward & occupied positions in T.15. Advance on this axis thereafter supported from here 13.05 hrs (C/78) LOCQUIGNOL	
		15.00	C/H INF (20 Bn 2) held up by MG FIRE in LOCQUIGNOL	
FOTOY	5th	05.30	21st Div. to take over & passed through 17 Div. Command of Artillery taken over by CRA 21st Div. 78 Bde. moved forward to positions of readiness in area of LA-TETE-NOIRE. Battn. remained in position until other 21 DA.	29/1
"	6th		" " "	19/1
LA-TETE-NOIRE	7th		O.C. 12 C.O.O. INF. ackn in support line U.23.C.6.0 — U.12.C.0.0. INF. made good progress. A.t.C. Battalion crossed SAMBRE & took up position of readiness in U.16d. Remainder B & E (incl. &C in U.16 but advance continued to V.22b + V.16d where Battn. came into action.	19/1
MONT FONTAINE	8th			19/1

Army Form C. 2118

WAR DIARY
or
INTELLIGENCE SUMMARY
(Erase heading not required.)

R.E. BELGIUM & PART OF FRANCE
SHEET 81. 1:40,000.

J.E. BOE. R.F.A.

Instructions regarding War Diaries and Intelligence Summaries are contained in F. S. Regs., Part II and the Staff Manual respectively. Title Pages will be prepared in manuscript.

Place	Date Nov 1918	Hour	Summary of Events and Information	Remarks and references to Appendices
MONT-FONTAINE	9th		Advance of INF entered with little opposition. BDE moved + remain in LIMONT - FONTAINE AREA	AG1
	10th		All MLs closed up to LIMONT - FONTAINE. Nothing to record	AG2
	11th		Cessation of Hostilities at 11.0 a.m	
	13th		night march from Limont-Fontaine to Eugghies on role for Bus Area	
	14th		march to Elouges	
	15th		" " Hensies	
HAVRÉCOURT			Bde inspected by Maj-Gen. Sir Rob. Robertson GOC 17 Div.	

Casualties during month
Killed Officers NIL O. Ranks 4
Wounded " 1 O. Ranks 10.

Amm" Expended
15840 1896
4115   4.5 H.

[signature] Major
[signature] Capt. Adjt.
18th Bde RFA

Army Form C. 2118

WAR DIARY
or
INTELLIGENCE SUMMARY

(Erase heading not required.)

78th Bde RFA

Instructions regarding War Diaries and Intelligence Summaries are contained in F.S. Regs., Part II. and the Staff Manual respectively. Title Pages will be prepared in manuscript.

Place	Date Dec 1918	Hour	Summary of Events and Information	Remarks and references to Appendices
			REF. MAP FRANCE SHEETS VALENCIENNES 12, LENS 11, ABBEVILLE 14. 1/100,000	
HAVCOURT	1-3		Nothing to report.	A/M
do	4		Representative parade 8 Bde to H.M. The King near Neuvilly - 11.00 hrs. (NEUVILLY)	A/M
do	5+6		Nothing	A/M
"	7		Marched to MANANCOURT.	A/M
MANANCOURT	8		do. MEAULTE	A/M
MEAULTE	9		do PONT NOYELLES	A/M
PONT NOYELLES	10		do. ALLERY	A/M
ALLERY	11-31		Nothing to report. Casualties - nil	

Above Lt Col CAM RA
for OC 78 Bde RFA

WAR DIARY
or
INTELLIGENCE SUMMARY

Army Form C. 2118

78 Bn[jade] RFA

MAP FRANCE SHEET DIEPPE 16 1/100,000

Vol 43 RM

Place	Date	Hour	Summary of Events and Information	Remarks and references to Appendices
ALLERY	January 1919	Nothing	Demobilised during month. 2 Officers 72 ORs	

Alex McCammat
for O.C. 78 Bde RFA.

Army Form C. 2118

WAR DIARY
or
INTELLIGENCE SUMMARY
(Erase heading not required.)

78 Bde RFA

Place	Date	Hour	Summary of Events and Information	Remarks and references to Appendices
ALLERY	Feby. 1919.		REF. MAP FRANCE SHEET DIEPPE 16 (1/100.000)	
	1-24		Nothing.	
	25th		Guns & ammunition wagons shipped east to Base Park LONGPRÉ.	Wpl 44
	25-28		Nothing	
			Number demobilised during month.	
			2 Officers	
			91 ORs.	
				Alex ?? Adm + ad
				t o c 78 Bde RFA.

WAR DIARY
or
INTELLIGENCE SUMMARY

Army Form C. 2118

78 Bde RFA

Sheet DIEPPE 16 1/100,000

Place	Date	Hour	Summary of Events and Information	Remarks and references to Appendices
ALLERY (SOMME)	March 1-31 1919		Nothing to report. Mules demobilised during month. Officers nil OR's 45	Nil 4 5

Alex Bn
Mr or 78 Bde RFA

www.ingramcontent.com/pod-product-compliance
Lightning Source LLC
Chambersburg PA
CBHW080854230426
43662CB00013B/2103